Cram101 Textbook Outlines to accompany:

One and Several Variables: Calculus

Salas, Hille & Hetgen, 9th Edition

D1401811

AUG 2 - 2011

You have a discounted membership at www.Cram101.com with this book.

Get all of the practice tests for the chapters of this textbook, and access in-depth reference material for writing essays and papers. Here is an example from a Cram101 Biology text:

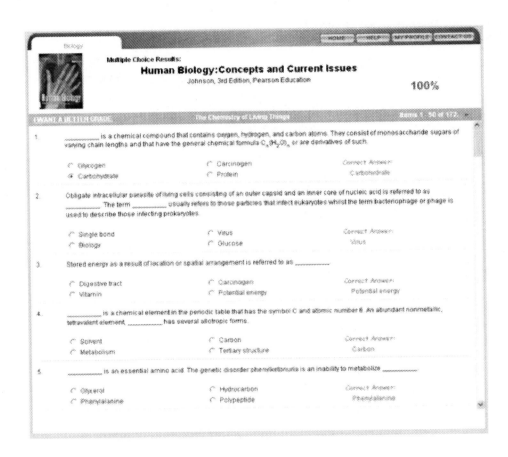

When you need problem solving help with math, stats, and other disciplines, www.Cram101.com will walk through the formulas and solutions step by step.

With Cram101.com online, you also have access to extensive reference material.

You will nail those essays and papers. Here is an example from a Cram101 Biology text:

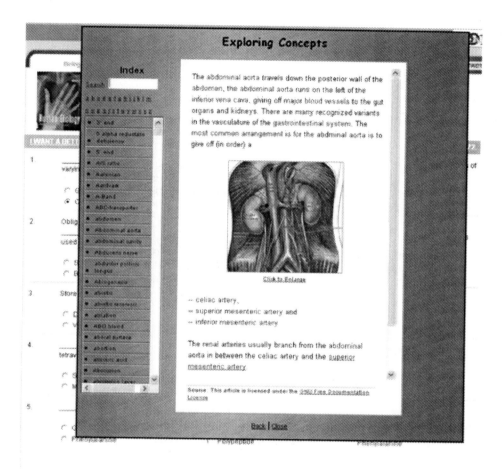

Learning System

Cram101 Textbook Outlines is a learning system. The notes in this book are the highlights of your textbook, you will never have to highlight a book again.

How to use this book. Take this book to class, it is your notebook for the lecture. The notes and highlights on the left hand side of the pages follow the outline and order of the textbook. All you have to do is follow along while your intructor presents the lecture. Circle the items emphasized in class and add other important information on the right side. With Cram101 Textbook Outlines you'll spend less time writing and more time listening. Learning becomes more efficient.

Cram101.com Online

Increase your studying efficiency by using Cram101.com's practice tests and online reference material. It is the perfect complement to Cram101 Textbook Outlines. Use self-teaching matching tests or simulate in-class testing with comprehensive multiple choice tests, or simply use Cram's true and false tests for quick review. Cram101.com even allows you to enter your in-class notes for an integrated studying format combining the textbook notes with your class notes.

Visit **www.Cram101.com**, click Sign Up at the top of the screen, and enter **DK73DW1881** in the promo code box on the registration screen. Access to www.Cram101.com is normally $9.95, but because you have purchased this book, your access fee is only $4.95. Sign up and stop highlighting textbooks forever.

One and Several Variables: Calculus
Salas, Hille & Hetgen, 9th

CONTENTS

Calculus	Calculus is a mathematical subject that includes the study of limits, derivatives, integrals, and power series and constitutes a major part of modern university curriculum.
Counting	Counting is the mathematical action of repeatedly adding or subtracting one, usually to find out how many objects there are or to set aside a desired number of objects.
Roman	Roman numerals are a numeral system originating in ancient Rome, adapted from Etruscan numerals.
Mean	The mean, the average in everyday English, which is also called the arithmetic mean (and is distinguished from the geometric mean or harmonic mean). The average is also called the sample mean. The expected value of a random variable, which is also called the population mean.
Trigonometry	Trigonometry is a branch of mathematics which deals with triangles, particularly triangles in a plane where one angle of the triangle is 90 degrees, and a variety of other topological relations such as spheres, in other branches, such as spherical trigonometry.
Algebra	Algebra is a branch of mathematics concerning the study of structure, relation and quantity.
Origin	In mathematics, the origin of a coordinate system is the point where the axes of the system intersect.
Tangent	In trigonometry, the tangent is a function defined as $\tan x = {\sin x}/{\cos x}$. The function is so-named because it can be defined as the length of a certain segment of a tangent (in the geometric sense) to the unit circle. In plane geometry, a line is tangent to a curve, at some point, if both line and curve pass through the point with the same direction.
Scratch	Scratch is an interpreted dynamic visual programming language based on Squeak, a smalltalk implementation directly derived from Smalltalk-80.
Notation	Mathematical notation is used to represent ideas.
Newton	Sir Isaac Newton, was an English physicist, mathematician, astronomer, natural philosopher, and alchemist, regarded by many as the greatest figure in the history of science
Leibniz	Leibniz was a German mathematician and philosopher. He invented calculus independently of Newton, and his notation is the one in general use since.
Isaac Newton	Sir Isaac Newton was an English physicist, mathematician, astronomer, natural philosopher, and alchemist, regarded by many as the greatest figure in the history of science.
Turn	A turn is 360° or 2δ radians.
Light	Light is electromagnetic radiation with a wavelength that is visible to the eye (visible light) or, in a technical or scientific context, electromagnetic radiation of any wavelength.
Development	In mathematics, a development is a countable collection of open covers of a topological space that satisfies certain separation axioms.
Theoretical	In mathematics, the word theoretical is used informally to refer to certain distinct bodies of knowledge about mathematics.
Element	An element or member of a set is an object that when collected together make up the set.
Elements	In mathematics, the elements , or members of a set or more generally a class are all those objects which when collected together make up the set or class.
Number system	number system is a set of numbers, in the broadest sense of the word, together with one or more operations, such as addition or multiplication.
Real number	In mathematics, a real number may be described informally as a number that can be given by an infinite decimal representation.
Multiplication	In mathematics, multiplication is an elementary arithmetic operation. When one of the numbers is a whole number, multiplication is the repeated sum of the other number.

Go to **Cram101.com** for the Practice Tests for this Chapter.

Arithmetic	Arithmetic or arithmetics is the oldest and most elementary branch of mathematics, used by almost everyone, for tasks ranging from simple daily counting to advanced science and business calculations.
Arithmetic operations	The traditional arithmetic operations are addition, subtraction, multiplication and division, although more advanced operations (such as manipulations of percentages, square root, exponentiation, and logarithmic functions) are also sometimes included in this subject.
Numerator	A numerator is a numeral used to indicate a count. The most common use of the word today is to name the part of a fraction that tells the number or count of equal parts.
Rational	In mathematics, a rational number is a number which can be expressed as a ratio of two integers. Non-integer rational numbers (commonly called fractions) are usually written as the vulgar fraction a / b, where b is not zero.
Expansion	An expansion of a product of sums expresses it as a sum of products by using the fact that multiplication distributes over addition.
Denominator	A denominator is the part of a fraction that tells how many equal parts make up a whole, and which is used in the name of the fraction: "halves", "thirds", "fourths" or "quarters", "fifths" and so on.
Irrational	In mathematics, an irrational number is any real number that is not a rational number- that is, it is a number which cannot be expressed as a fraction m/n, where m and n are integers.
Irrational number	In mathematics, an irrational number is any real number that is not a rational number ¡ª that is, it is a number which cannot be expressed as m/n, where m and n are integers.
Negative number	A negative number is a number that is less than zero.
Units	The units of measurement are a globally standardized and modernized form of the metric system.
Coordinate	A coordinate is a set of numbers that designate location in a given reference system, such as x,y in a planar coordinate system or an x,y,z in a three-dimensional coordinate system.
Number line	A number line is a one-dimensional picture in which the integers are shown as specially-marked points evenly spaced on a line.
Symbols	Symbols are objects, characters, or other concrete representations of ideas, concepts, or other abstractions.
Inequality	In mathematics, an inequality is a statement about the relative size or order of two objects.
Magnitude	The magnitude of a mathematical object is its size: a property by which it can be larger or smaller than other objects of the same kind; in technical terms, an ordering of the class of objects to which it belongs.
Absolute value	In mathematics, the absolute value (or modulus) of a real number is its numerical value without regard to its sign.
Endpoint	In geometry, an endpoint is a point at which a line segment or ray terminates.
Interval	In elementary algebra, an interval is a set that contains every real number between two indicated numbers and may contain the two numbers themselves.
Sum	A sum is the result of the addition of a set of numbers. The numbers may be natural numbers, complex numbers, matrices, or still more complicated objects. An infinite sum is a subtle procedure known as a series.
Square	In plane geometry, a square is a polygon with four equal sides, four right angles, and parallel opposite sides. In algebra, the square of a number is that number multiplied by itself.
Interval notation	Interval notation is the notation in which permitted values for a variable are expressed as ranging over a certain interval; "5 < x < 9" is an example of the application of interval notation.

Solid	In mathematics, solid geometry was the traditional name for the geometry of three-dimensional Euclidean space — for practical purposes the kind of space we live in.
Infinity	Infinity is the state of being greater than any finite number, however large.
Minus	The plus and minus signs are mathematical symbols used to represent the notions of positive and negative as well as the operations of addition and subtraction.
Upper bound	In mathematics, especially in order theory, an upper bound of a subset S of some partially ordered set is an element of P which is greater than or equal to every element of S.
Lower bound	The term lower bound is defined dually as an element of P which is lesser than or equal to every element of S.
Bounded	In mathematical analysis and related areas of mathematics, a set is called bounded, if it is, in a certain sense, of finite size.
Root	In mathematics, a root of a complex-valued function f is a member x of the domain of f such that f(x) vanishes at x, that is, $x : f(x) = 0$.
Quadratic equation	In mathematics, a quadratic equation is a polynomial equation of the second degree. The general form is $ax^2 + bx + c = 0$.
Quadratic formula	A quadratic equation with real solutions, called roots, which may be real or complex, is given by the quadratic formula: $x = \dfrac{-b \pm \sqrt{b^2 - 4ac}}{2a}$.
Statement	In common philosophical language, a proposition or statement, is the content of an assertion, that is, it is true-or-false and defined by the meaning of a particular piece of language.
Integers	The integers are the only integral domain whose positive elements are well-ordered, and in which order is preserved by addition. Like the natural numbers, the integers form a countably infinite set. The set of all integers is usually denoted in mathematics by a boldface Z .
Expression	An expression is a combination of numbers, operators, grouping symbols and/or free variables and bound variables arranged in a meaningful way which can be evaluated..
Product	In mathematics, a product is the result of multiplying, or an expression that identifies factors to be multiplied.
Common Factor	common Factor is the largest positive integer that divides both numbers without remainder.
Factors	In mathematics, factorization (British English: factorisation) or factoring is the decomposition of an object (for example, a number, a polynomial, or a matrix) into a product of other objects, or factors, which when multiplied together give the original.
Divisor	In mathematics, a divisor of an integer n, also called a factor of n, is an integer which evenly divides n without leaving a remainder.
Rectangle	In geometry, a rectangle is defined as a quadrilateral where all four of its angles are right angles.
Perimeter	Perimeter is the distance around a given two-dimensional object. As a general rule, the perimeter of a polygon can always be calculated by adding all the length of the sides together. So, the formula for triangles is $P = a + b + c$, where a, b and c stand for each side of it. For quadrilaterals the equation is $P = a + b + c + d$. For equilateral polygons, $P = na$, where n is the number of sides and a is the side length.
Circle	In Euclidean geometry, a circle is the set of all points in a plane at a fixed distance, called the radius, from a given point, the center.
Conjecture	In mathematics, a conjecture is a mathematical statement which appears likely to be true, but has not

been formally proven to be true under the rules of mathematical logic.

Terminating	A Terminating decimal is a decimal fraction which ends after a definite number of digits.
Solution set	A solution set is a set of possible values that a variable can take on in order to satisfy a given set of conditions, which may include equations and inequalities.
Repeating	A repeating decimal is a number whose decimal representation eventually becomes periodic (i.e. the same number sequence repeating indefinitely).
Repeating decimals	Recurring or repeating decimals are numbers which when expressed as decimals have a set of "final" digits which repeat an infinite number of times.
Triangle	A triangle is one of the basic shapes of geometry: a polygon with three vertices and three sides which are straight line segments.
Triangle inequality	Triangle inequality is the theorem stating that for any triangle, the measure of a given side must be less than the sum of the other two sides but greater than the difference between the two sides.
Union	In set theory and other branches of mathematics, the union of a collection of sets is the set that contains everything that belongs to any of the sets, but nothing else.
Analogy	Analogy is bother the congnitive process of transferring information from a particular subject , and a linguistic expression corresponding to such a process.
Nonnegative	The nonnegative integers are all the integers from zero on upwards.
Arithmetic mean	Arithmetic mean of a list of numbers is the sum of all the members of the list divided by the number of items in the list.
Coordinate system	In mathematics and its applications, a coordinate system is a system for assigning an n-tuple of numbers or scalars to each point in an n-dimensional space.
Analytic geometry	Analytic geometry is the study of geometry using the principles of algebra. Analytic geometry can be explained more simply: it is concerned with defining geometrical shapes in a numerical way and extracting numerical information from that representation.
Plane	In mathematics, a plane is a two-dimensional manifold or surface that is perfectly flat.
Perpendicular	In geometry, two lines or planes if one falls on the other in such a way as to create congruent adjacent angles. The term may be used as a noun or adjective. Thus, referring to Figure 1, the line AB is the perpendicular to CD through the point B.
Axes	An axes is when two lines intersect somewhere on a plane creating a right angle at intersection
Horizontal	In astronomy, geography, geometry and related sciences and contexts, a plane is said to be horizontal at a given point if it is locally perpendicular to the gradient of the gravity field, i.e., with the direction of the gravitational force at that point.
Axis	An axis is a straight line around which a geometric figure can be rotated.
Quadrant	A Quadrant consists of one quarter of the coordinate plane.
Ordered pair	An ordered pair is a collection of two not necessarily distinct objects, one of which is distinguished as the first coordinate and the other as the second coordinate.
Ordinate	The Ordinate is the y- coordinate of a point within a two dimensional coordinate system. It is sometimes used to refer to the axis rather than the distance along the coordinate system.
Cartesian	Cartesian means of or relating to the French philosopher and mathematician RenÃ© Descartes.
Cartesian coordinate system	In mathematics, the Cartesian coordinate system is used to determine each point uniquely in a plane through two numbers, usually called the x-coordinate and the y-coordinate of the point.

Go to **Cram101.com** for the Practice Tests for this Chapter.

Descartes	Descartes was a highly influential French philosopher, mathematician, scientist, and writer. Dubbed the "Founder of Modern Philosophy", and the "Father of Modern Mathematics". His theories provided the basis for the calculus of Newton and Leibniz, by applying infinitesimal calculus to the tangent line problem, thus permitting the evolution of that branch of modern mathematics
Abscissa	Abscissa consists of the first element in a coordinate pair. When graphed in the coordinate plane, it is the distance from the y-axis. Frequently called the x coordinate.
Midpoint	midpoint is the middle point of a line segment.
Undefined	In mathematics, defined and undefined are used to explain whether or not expressions have meaningful, sensible, and unambiguous values.
Slope	Slope is often used to describe the measurement of the steepness, incline, gradient, or grade of a straight line. The slope is defined as the ratio of the "rise" divided by the "run" between two points on a line, or in other words, the ratio of the altitude change to the horizontal distance between any two points on the line.
Trigonometric	In mathematics, the trigonometric functions are functions of an angle; they are important when studying triangles and modeling periodic phenomena, among many other applications.
Trigonometric functions	The trigonometric functions are functions of an angle; they are important when studying triangles and modeling periodic phenomena, among many other applications.
Variable	A variable is a symbolic representation denoting a quantity or expression. It often represents an "unknown" quantity that has the potential to change.
Intercept	Any point where a graph makes contact with an coordinate axis is called an intercept of the graph
Function	The mathematical concept of a function expresses the intuitive idea of deterministic dependence between two quantities, one of which is viewed as primary and the other as secondary. A function then is a way to associate a unique output for each input of a specified type, for example, a real number or an element of a given set.
Intersecting	In geometry, intersecting lines are two lines that share one or more common points.
Parallel lines	The existence and properties of parallel lines are the basis of Euclid's parallel postulate. Parallel lines are two lines on the same plane that do not intersect even assuming that lines extend to infinity in either direction.
Intersection	In mathematics, the intersection of two sets A and B is the set that contains all elements of A that also belong to B (or equivalently, all elements of B that also belong to A), but no other elements.
Graphs	Graphs are the basic objects of study in graph theory. Informally speaking, a graph is a set of objects called points, nodes, or vertices connected by links called lines or edges.
Conic	In mathematics, a conic section is a curve that can be formed by intersecting a cone with a plane.
Ellipse	In mathematics, an ellipse .
Segment	In geometry, a line segment is a part of a line that is bounded by two end points, and contains every point on the line between its end points.
Line segment	A line segment is a part of a line that is bounded by two end points, and contains every point on the line between its end points.
Vertex	In geometry, a vertex is a special kind of point, usually a corner of a polygon, polyhedron, or higher dimensional polytope. In the geometry of curves a vertex is a point of where the first derivative of curvature is zero. In graph theory, a vertex is the fundamental unit out of which graphs are formed
Center	In geometry, the center of an object is a point in some sense in the middle of the object.
Radius	In classical geometry, a radius of a circle or sphere is any line segment from its center to its

Go to Cram101.com for the Practice Tests for this Chapter.

boundary. By extension, the radius of a circle or sphere is the length of any such segment. The radius is half the diameter. In science and engineering the term radius of curvature is commonly used as a synonym for radius.

Parabola	In mathematics, the parabola is a conic section generated by the intersection of a right circular conical surface and a plane parallel to a generating straight line of that surface. It can also be defined as locus of points in a plane which are equidistant from a given point.
Hyperbola	In mathematics, a hyperbola is a type of conic section defined as the intersection between a right circular conical surface and a plane which cuts through both halves of the cone.
Tangent line	Tangent line has two distinct but etymologically-related meanings: one in geometry and one in trigonometry.
Right triangle	Right triangle has one 90° internal angle a right angle.
Isosceles	An Isosceles triange is a triangle with at least two sides of equal length.
Equilateral	In geometry, an equilateral polygon is a polygon which has all sides of the same length.
Equilateral triangle	An Equilateral Triangle is a triangle in which all sides are of equal length.
Hypotenuse	The hypotenuse of a right triangle is the triangle's longest side; the side opposite the right angle.
Centroid	In geometry, the centroid or barycenter of an object X in n-dimensional space is the intersection of all hyperplanes that divide X into two parts of equal moment about the hyperplane
Median	In probability theory and statistics, a median is a number dividing the higher half of a sample, a population, or a probability distribution from the lower half.
Parallelogram	A parallelogram is a four-sided plane figure that has two sets of opposite parallel sides.
Quadrilateral	A quadrilateral is a polygon with four sides and four vertices.
Adjacent	In geometry, adjacent angles are angles that have a common ray coming out of the vertex going between two other rays.
Fahrenheit	Fahrenheit is a temperature scale named after the German physicist Daniel Gabriel Fahrenheit , who proposed it in 1724.
Linear	The word linear comes from the Latin word linearis, which means created by lines.
Celsius	Celsius is, or relates to, the Celsius temperature scale .
Degree	In mathematics, there are several meanings of degree depending on the subject.
Temperature	Temperature is a physical property of a system that underlies the common notions of hot and cold; something that is hotter has the greater temperature.
Integration	Integration is a process of combining or accumulating. It may also refer to:
Differential calculus	Differential calculus, a field in mathematics, is the study of how functions change when their inputs change. The primary object of study in differential calculus is the derivative.
Range	In mathematics, the range of a function is the set of all "output" values produced by that function. Given a function f :A face="symbol">® B, the range of f, is defined to be the set {x B:x= class=Unicode >f(a) for some a class="unicode"> A}.
Domain	In mathematics, a domain of a k-place relation L X_1

Go to **Cram101.com** for the Practice Tests for this Chapter.

class="unicode">× … × X_k is one of the sets
X_j, 1 ≤ j ≤ k. In the special case
where k = 2 and L X_1 ×
X_2 is a function L : $X_1 \rightarrow X_2$, it is
conventional to refer to X_1 as the domain of the function and to refer to X_2 as
the codomain of the function.

Image
In mathematics, image is a part of the set theoretic notion of function.

Independent variable
In mathematics, an independent variable is any of the arguments, i.e. "inputs", to a function. Thus if we have a function f(x), then x is a independent variable.

Dependent variable
In a function the dependent variable, is the variable which is the value, i.e. the "output", of the function.

Graph of a function
In mathematics, the graph of a function f is the collection of all ordered pairs . In particular, graph means the graphical representation of this collection, in the form of a curve or surface, together with axes, etc. Graphing on a Cartesian plane is sometimes referred to as curve sketching.

Curve
In mathematics, the concept of a curve tries to capture the intuitive idea of a geometrical one-dimensional and continuous object. A simple example is the circle.

Symmetry
Symmetry means "constancy", i.e. if something retains a certain feature even after we change a way of looking at it, then it is symmetric.

Even function
Even function are functions which satisfy particular symmetry relations, with respect to taking additive inverses.

Reciprocal
In mathematics, the multiplicative inverse of a number x, denoted 1/x or x^{-1}, is the number which, when multiplied by x, yields 1. The multiplicative inverse of x is also called the reciprocal of

Cross section
In geometry, a cross section is the intersection of a body in 2-dimensional space with a line, or of a body in 3-dimensional space with a plane

Volume
The volume of a solid object is the three-dimensional concept of how much space it occupies, often quantified numerically.

Cylinder
In mathematics, a cylinder is a quadric surface, with the following equation in Cartesian coordinates: $(x/_a)^2 + (y/_b)^2 = 1$.

Lateral
A lateral surface is the surface or face of a solid on its sides. It can also be defined as any face or surface that is not a base.

Cube
A cube is a three-dimensional solid object bounded by six square faces, facets, or sides, with three meeting at each vertex.

Diagonal
A diagonal can refer to a line joining two nonadjacent vertices of a polygon or polyhedron, or in some contexts any upward or downward sloping line. .

Legs
In a right triangle, the legs of the triangle are the two sides that are perpendicular to each other, as opposed to the hypotenuse.

Cone
A cone is a three-dimensional geometric shape formed by straight lines through a fixed point (vertex) to the points of a fixed curve (directrix)

Feature
In geographic information systems, a feature comprises an entity with a geographic location, typically determined by points, arcs, or polygons. Carriageways and cadastres exemplify feature data.

Circumference
The circumference is the distance around a closed curve. Circumference is a kind of perimeter.

Sphere
In mathematics, a sphere is the set of all points in three-dimensional space (R^3) which are at distance r from a fixed point of that space, where r is a positive real number called the radius of

the sphere. The fixed point is called the center or centre, and is not part of the sphere itself.

Rational function
In mathematics, a rational function is any function which can be written as the ratio of two polynomial functions.

Exponential
In mathematics, exponential growth occurs when the growth rate of a function is always proportional to the function's current size.

Exponential function
Exponential function is one of the most important functions in mathematics. A function commonly used to study growth and decay

Logarithm
In mathematics, a logarithm of a number x is the exponent y of the power by such that x = b^y. The value used for the base b must be neither 0 nor 1, nor a root of 1 in the case of the extension to complex numbers, and is typically 10, e, or 2.

Polynomial
In mathematics, a polynomial is an expression that is constructed from one or more variables and constants, using only the operations of addition, subtraction, multiplication, and constant positive whole number exponents. is a polynomial. Note in particular that division by an expression containing a variable is not in general allowed in polynomials. [1]

Coefficient
In mathematics, a coefficient is a constant multiplicative factor of a certain object. The object can be such things as a variable, a vector, a function, etc. For example, the coefficient of $9x^2$ is 9.

Constant
In mathematics and the mathematical sciences, a constant is a fixed, but possibly unspecified, value. This is in contrast to a variable, which is not fixed.

Constant function
Constant function is a function whose values do not vary and thus are constant.

Factor theorem
The factor theorem is a theorem for finding out the factors of a polynomial.

Theorem
In mathematics, a theorem is a statement that can be proved on the basis of explicitly stated or previously agreed assumptions.

Linear function
A linear function is a first degree polynomial mathematical function of the form: f(x) = mx + b where m and b are real constants and x is a real variable.

Quadratic function
A quadratic function is a polynomial function of the form $f(x) = ax^2 + bx + c$, where a, b, c are real numbers and a , 0.

Shapes
Shapes are external two-dimensional outlines, with the appearance or configuration of some thing - in contrast to the matter or content or substance of which it is composed.

Vertical asymptote
Vertical asymptote is a straight line or curve A to which another curve B the one being studied approaches closer and closer as one moves along it.

Asymptote
An asymptote is a straight line or curve A to which another curve B approaches closer and closer as one moves along it. As one moves along B, the space between it and the asymptote A becomes smaller and
smaller, and can in fact be made as small as one could wish by going far enough along. A curve may or may not touch or cross its asymptote. In fact, the curve may intersect the asymptote an infinite number of times.

Ray
A ray given two distinct points A and B on the ray, is the set of points C on the line containing points A and B such that A is not strictly between C and B.

Coterminal
Initial objects are also called coterminal, and terminal objects are also called final.

Measure
A measure is a function that assigns a number to subsets of a given set.

Rotation
A rotation is a movement of an object in a circular motion. A two-dimensional object rotates around a center (or point) of rotation. A three-dimensional object rotates around a line called an axis. If the

Go to **Cram101.com** for the Practice Tests for this Chapter.
And, **NEVER** highlight a book again!

axis of rotation is within the body, the body is said to rotate upon itself, or spin—which implies relative speed and perhaps free-movement with angular momentum. A circular motion about an external point, e.g. the Earth about the Sun, is called an orbit or more properly an orbital revolution.

Radian

The radian is a unit of plane angle. It is represented by the symbol "rad" or, more rarely, by the superscript c (for "circular measure"). For example, an angle of 1.2 radians would be written "1.2 rad" or "1.2c" (second symbol can produce confusion with centigrads).

Radian measure

radian measure is a unit of plane angle, equal to 180/ð degrees, or about 57.2958 degrees

Cosecant

Cosecant is a term in Trigonometry used to describe the secant of the complement of a cirlce.

Cotangent

Cotangent is the ratio of the adjacent to the opposite side of a right-angeled triangle

Sine

Sine is a trigonemtric function that is important when studying triangles and modeling periodic phenomena, among other applications.

Cosine

The cosine of an angle is the ratio of the length of the adjacent side to the length of the hypotenuse.

Secant

Secant is a trigonometric function that is the reciprocal of cosine.

Period

In business, particularly accounting, a period is the time intervals that the accounts, statement, payments, or other calculations cover.

Ratio

A ratio is a quantity that denotes the proportional amount or magnitude of one quantity relative to another.

Opposite

In mathematics, the additive inverse, or opposite of a number n is the number that, when added to n, yields zero. The additive inverse of n is denoted −n. For example, 7 is −7, because 7 + (−7) = 0, and the additive inverse of −0.3 is 0.3, because −0.3 + 0.3 = 0.

Additive inverse

In mathematics, the additive inverse of a number n is the number that, when added to n, yields zero. The additive inverse of n is denoted −n. For example, 7 is −7, because 7 + (−7) = 0, and the additive inverse of −0.3 is 0.3, because −0.3 + 0.3 = 0.

Law of cosines

The law of cosines is a statement about a general triangle which relates the lengths of its sides to the cosine of one of its angles.

Trace

In linear algebra, the trace of an n-by-n square matrix A is defined to be the sum of the elements on the main diagonal of A,

Right angle

In geometry and trigonometry, a right angle is defined as an angle between two straight intersecting lines of ninety degrees, or one-quarter of a circle.

Unit circle

Unit circle is a circle with a unit radius, i.e., a circle whose radius is 1.

Equivalent

Equivalence is the condition of being equivalent or essentially equal.

Law of sines

If the sides of the triangle are a, b and c and the angles opposite those sides are A, B and C, then the law of sines states:a/sin A=b/sin B=c/sin C=2R where R is the radius of the triangle face=symbol>¢s circumcircle.

Greater than

In mathematics, an inequality is a statement about the relative size or order of two objects. For example 14 > 10, or 14 is greater than 10.

Quartic

In mathematics and elsewhere, the adjective quartic means fourth order, such as the function x4. A quartic number is a number which equals the fourth power of an integer.

Quotient

In mathematics, a quotient is the end result of a division problem. It can also be expressed as the number of times the divisor divides into the dividend.

Combination

In combinatorial mathematics, a combination is an un-ordered collection of unique elements.

Composition

In mathematics, a composition of a positive integer n is a way of writing n as a sum of positive

	integers.
Power	Power has many meanings, most of which simply .
Proof	In mathematics, a proof is a demonstration that, assuming certain axioms, some statement is necessarily true.
Mathematical induction	Mathematical induction is a method of mathematical proof typically used to establish that a given statement is true of all natural numbers
Column	In mathematics, a matrix can be thought of as each row or column being a vector. Hence, a space formed by row vectors or column vectors are said to be a row space or a column space.
Euclid	Euclid, also known as Euclid of Alexandria, was a Greek mathematician. His Elements is the most successful textbook in the history of mathematics. In it, the principles of geometry are deduced from a small set of axioms. His method of proving mathematical theorems by logical reasoning from accepted first principles remains the backbone of mathematics and is responsible for the field face=symbol>¢s characteristic rigor
Aristotle	Aristotle was a Greek philosopher, a student of Plato and teacher of Alexander the Great. He wrote on diverse subjects, including physics, metaphysics, poetry, biology and zoology, logic, rhetoric, politics, government, and ethics.
Hypothesis	A hypothesis consists either of a suggested explanation for a phenomenon or of a reasoned proposal suggesting a possible correlation between multiple phenomena.
Conclusion	In a mathematical proof or a syllogism, a conclusion is a statement that is the logical consequence of preceding statements.
Converse	Converse Logic is a concept in traditional logic referring to a "type of immediate inference in which from a given proposition another proposition is inferred which has as its subject the predicate of the original proposition and as its predicate the subject of the original proposition (the quality of the proposition being retained)."
Axiom	An axiom is any starting assumption from which other statements are logically derived
Factoring	In mathematics, Factoring is the decomposition of an object into a product of other objects, or factors, which when multiplied together give the original.
Convex	A convex function curves downwards. The graph of a convex function of one variable remains above its tangents and below its cords.
Convex polygon	In geometry, a convex polygon is a simple polygon whose interior is a convex set.
Subset	A subset is a set whose members are members of another set or a set contained within another set.
Subsets	Subsets are groups whose members are members of another set or a set contained within another set.
Polygon	In geometry a polygon is a plane figure that is bounded by a closed path or circuit, composed of a finite number of sequential line segments.
Interior angle	An interior angle is an angle formed by two sides of a simple polygon that share an endpoint, namely, the angle on the inner side of the polygon.
Empty	In mathematics and more specifically set theory, the empty set is the unique set which contains no elements.

Calculus	Calculus is a mathematical subject that includes the study of limits, derivatives, integrals, and power series and constitutes a major part of modern university curriculum.
Rectangle	In geometry, a rectangle is defined as a quadrilateral where all four of its angles are right angles.
Sum	A sum is the result of the addition of a set of numbers. The numbers may be natural numbers, complex numbers, matrices, or still more complicated objects. An infinite sum is a subtle procedure known as a series.
Mean	The mean, the average in everyday English, which is also called the arithmetic mean (and is distinguished from the geometric mean or harmonic mean). The average is also called the sample mean. The expected value of a random variable, which is also called the population mean.
Function	The mathematical concept of a function expresses the intuitive idea of deterministic dependence between two quantities, one of which is viewed as primary and the other as secondary. A function then is a way to associate a unique output for each input of a specified type, for example, a real number or an element of a given set.
Graph of a function	In mathematics, the graph of a function f is the collection of all ordered pairs . In particular, graph means the graphical representation of this collection, in the form of a curve or surface, together with axes, etc. Graphing on a Cartesian plane is sometimes referred to as curve sketching.
Curve	In mathematics, the concept of a curve tries to capture the intuitive idea of a geometrical one-dimensional and continuous object. A simple example is the circle.
Limit of a function	The limit of a function is a fundamental concept in analysis. Informally, a function f can be made as close to L as desired, by making x close enough to p.
Real number	In mathematics, a real number may be described informally as a number that can be given by an infinite decimal representation.
Negative number	A negative number is a number that is less than zero.
Greater than	In mathematics, an inequality is a statement about the relative size or order of two objects. For example 14 > 10, or 14 is greater than 10.
Rational	In mathematics, a rational number is a number which can be expressed as a ratio of two integers. Non-integer rational numbers (commonly called fractions) are usually written as the vulgar fraction a / b, where b is not zero.
Irrational	In mathematics, an irrational number is any real number that is not a rational number- that is, it is a number which cannot be expressed as a fraction m/n, where m and n are integers.
Irrational number	In mathematics, an irrational number is any real number that is not a rational number ¡ª that is, it is a number which cannot be expressed as m/n, where m and n are integers.
Irrational numbers	In mathematics, Irrational numbers are any real number that is not a rational number ¡ª that is, it is a number which cannot be expressed as m/n, where m and n are integers.
Ratio	A ratio is a quantity that denotes the proportional amount or magnitude of one quantity relative to another.
Quotient	In mathematics, a quotient is the end result of a division problem. It can also be expressed as the number of times the divisor divides into the dividend.
Radian	The radian is a unit of plane angle. It is represented by the symbol "rad" or, more rarely, by the superscript c (for "circular measure"). For example, an angle of 1.2 radians would be written "1.2 rad" or "1.2c" (second symbol can produce confusion with centigrads).

Go to **Cram101.com** for the Practice Tests for this Chapter.

Go to **Cram101.com** for the Practice Tests for this Chapter.
And, **NEVER** highlight a book again!

Radian measure	radian measure is a unit of plane angle, equal to 180/ð degrees, or about 57.2958 degrees
Measure	A measure is a function that assigns a number to subsets of a given set.
Slope	Slope is often used to describe the measurement of the steepness, incline, gradient, or grade of a straight line. The slope is defined as the ratio of the "rise" divided by the "run" between two points on a line, or in other words, the ratio of the altitude change to the horizontal distance between any two points on the line.
Limiting	limiting Any process by which a specified characteristic usually amplitude of the output of a device is prevented from exceeding a predetermined value.
Secant	Secant is a trigonometric function that is the reciprocal of cosine.
Secant line	secant line of a curve is a line that intersects two or more points on the curve.
Tangent	In trigonometry, the tangent is a function defined as $\tan x = {}^{\sin x}/_{\cos x}$. The function is so-named because it can be defined as the length of a certain segment of a tangent (in the geometric sense) to the unit circle. In plane geometry, a line is tangent to a curve, at some point, if both line and curve pass through the point with the same direction.
Tangent line	Tangent line has two distinct but etymologically-related meanings: one in geometry and one in trigonometry.
Experiment	In the scientific method, an experiment (Latin: ex-+-periri, "of (or from) trying"), is a set of actions and observations, performed in the context of solving a particular problem or question, in order to support or falsify a hypothesis or research concerning phenomena.
Interval	In elementary algebra, an interval is a set that contains every real number between two indicated numbers and may contain the two numbers themselves.
Constant	In mathematics and the mathematical sciences, a constant is a fixed, but possibly unspecified, value. This is in contrast to a variable, which is not fixed.
Argument	In mathematics, science including computer science, linguistics and engineering, an argument is, generally speaking, an independent variable or input to a function.
Inequality	In mathematics, an inequality is a statement about the relative size or order of two objects.
Absolute value	In mathematics, the absolute value (or modulus) of a real number is its numerical value without regard to its sign.
Proof	In mathematics, a proof is a demonstration that, assuming certain axioms, some statement is necessarily true.
Determining	Determining the expected value of a random variable displays the average or central value of the variable.It is a summary value of the distribution of the variable.
Conclusion	In a mathematical proof or a syllogism, a conclusion is a statement that is the logical consequence of preceding statements.
Graphs	Graphs are the basic objects of study in graph theory. Informally speaking, a graph is a set of objects called points, nodes, or vertices connected by links called lines or edges.
Horizontal	In astronomy, geography, geometry and related sciences and contexts, a plane is said to be horizontal at a given point if it is locally perpendicular to the gradient of the gravity field, i.e., with the direction of the gravitational force at that point.
Converse	Converse Logic is a concept in traditional logic referring to a "type of immediate inference in which from a given proposition another proposition is inferred which has as its subject the predicate of the original proposition and as its predicate the subject of the original

Go to **Cram101.com** for the Practice Tests for this Chapter.

Go to **Cram101.com** for the Practice Tests for this Chapter.
And, **NEVER** highlight a book again!

proposition (the quality of the proposition being retained)."

Theorem	In mathematics, a theorem is a statement that can be proved on the basis of explicitly stated or previously agreed assumptions.
Mathematical induction	Mathematical induction is a method of mathematical proof typically used to establish that a given statement is true of all natural numbers
Finite	In mathematics, a set is called finite if there is a bijection between the set and some set of the form {1, 2, ..., n} where n is a natural number.
Polynomial	In mathematics, a polynomial is an expression that is constructed from one or more variables and constants, using only the operations of addition, subtraction, multiplication, and constant positive whole number exponents. is a polynomial. Note in particular that division by an expression containing a variable is not in general allowed in polynomials. [1]
Continuous	A continuous function is a function for which, intuitively, small changes in the input result in small changes in the output.
Numerator	A numerator is a numeral used to indicate a count. The most common use of the word today is to name the part of a fraction that tells the number or count of equal parts.
Product	In mathematics, a product is the result of multiplying, or an expression that identifies factors to be multiplied.
Expression	An expression is a combination of numbers, operators, grouping symbols and/or free variables and bound variables arranged in a meaningful way which can be evaluated..
Central	Central is an adjective usually refering to being in the centre.
Difference quotient	The function difference divided by the point difference is known as the Difference quotient
Discontinuity	Continuous functions are of utmost importance in mathematics and applications. However, not all functions are continuous. If a function is not continuous at a point in its domain, one says that it has a discontinuity there. The set of all points of discontinuity of a function may be a discrete set, a dense set, or even the entire domain of the function.
Domain	In mathematics, a domain of a k-place relation L X_1 × ... × X_k is one of the sets X_i, 1 ≤ j ≤ k. In the special case where k = 2 and L X_1 class="unicode">× X_2 is a function L : X_1 class="unicode">→ X_2, it is conventional to refer to X_1 as the domain of the function and to refer to X_2 as the codomain of the function.
Infinite	infinite is the state of being greater than any finite real or natural number, however large.
Translation	In Euclidean geometry, a translation is moving every point a constant distance in a specified direction.
Direct	In mathematics and logic, a direct proof is a way of showing the truth or falsehood of a given statement by a straightforward combination of established facts, usually existing lemmas and theorems, without making any further assumptions.
Composite	A composite number is a positive integer which has a positive divisor other than one or itself.
Composite function	A composite function, formed by the composition of one function on another, represents the application of the former to the result of the application of the latter to the argument of the composite.

Go to **Cram101.com** for the Practice Tests for this Chapter.

Map	A map, is a symbolized depiction of space which highlights relations between components of that space. Most usually a map is a two-dimensional, geometrically accurate representation of a three-dimensional space.
Finite set	In mathematics, a finite set occurs if there is a bijection between the set and some set of the form 1, 2, ..., n where n is a natural number.
Squeeze Theorem	In calculus, the squeeze theorem is a theorem regarding the limit of a function. The theorem asserts that if two functions approach the same limit at a point, and if a third function is "squeezed" between those functions, then the third function also approaches that limit at that point.
Trigonometric	In mathematics, the trigonometric functions are functions of an angle; they are important when studying triangles and modeling periodic phenomena, among many other applications.
Trigonometric functions	The trigonometric functions are functions of an angle; they are important when studying triangles and modeling periodic phenomena, among many other applications.
Sine	Sine is a trigonemtric function that is important when studying triangles and modeling periodic phenomena, among other applications.
Continuous function	A continuous function is a function for which, intuitively, small changes in the input result in small changes in the output.
Root	In mathematics, a root of a complex-valued function f is a member x of the domain of f such that f(x) vanishes at x, that is, x : f (x) = 0.
Solution set	A solution set is a set of possible values that a variable can take on in order to satisfy a given set of conditions, which may include equations and inequalities.
Endpoint	In geometry, an endpoint is a point at which a line segment or ray terminates.
Rational function	In mathematics, a rational function is any function which can be written as the ratio of two polynomial functions.
Bounded	In mathematical analysis and related areas of mathematics, a set is called bounded, if it is, in a certain sense, of finite size.
Hypothesis	A hypothesis consists either of a suggested explanation for a phenomenon or of a reasoned proposal suggesting a possible correlation between multiple phenomena.
Identity	An identity is an equality that remains true regardless of the values of any variables that appear within it, to distinguish it from an equality which is true under more particular conditions.
Identity function	An identity function is a function that does not have any effect: it always returns the same value that was used as its argument.
Integers	The integers are the only integral domain whose positive elements are well-ordered, and in which order is preserved by addition. Like the natural numbers, the integers form a countably infinite set. The set of all integers is usually denoted in mathematics by a boldface Z .
Consecutive	Consecutive means in succession or back-to-back
Range	In mathematics, the range of a function is the set of all "output" values produced by that function. Given a function f :A → B, the range of class="unicode">f, is defined to be the set {x class="unicode"> B:x= class="unicode">f(a) for some a class="unicode"> A}.

Go to **Cram101.com** for the Practice Tests for this Chapter.

Go to **Cram101.com** for the Practice Tests for this Chapter.
And, **NEVER** highlight a book again!

Cube	A cube is a three-dimensional solid object bounded by six square faces, facets, or sides, with three meeting at each vertex.
Cube root	A cube root of a number is a number a such that $a^3 = x$.
Degree	In mathematics, there are several meanings of degree depending on the subject.
Cubic equation	In mathematics, a cubic equation is a polynomial equation of the third degree.
Elevation	The elevation of a geographic location is its height above a fixed reference point, often the mean sea level.
Nonnegative	The nonnegative integers are all the integers from zero on upwards.
Nth root	An nth root of a number a is a number b such that $b^n = a$.
Temperature	Temperature is a physical property of a system that underlies the common notions of hot and cold; something that is hotter has the greater temperature.
Meter	The metre (or meter, see spelling differences) is a measure of length. It is the basic unit of length in the metric system and in the International System of Units (SI), used around the world for general and scientific purposes.
Equator	The equator is an imaginary line on the Earth's surface equidistant from the North Pole and South Pole.
Opposite	In mathematics, the additive inverse, or opposite of a number n is the number that, when added to n, yields zero. The additive inverse of n is denoted −n. For example, 7 is −7, because 7 + (−7) = 0, and the additive inverse of −0.3 is 0.3, because −0.3 + 0.3 = 0.
Additive inverse	In mathematics, the additive inverse of a number n is the number that, when added to n, yields zero. The additive inverse of n is denoted −n. For example, 7 is −7, because 7 + (−7) = 0, and the additive inverse of −0.3 is 0.3, because −0.3 + 0.3 = 0.
Circle	In Euclidean geometry, a circle is the set of all points in a plane at a fixed distance, called the radius, from a given point, the center.
Radius	In classical geometry, a radius of a circle or sphere is any line segment from its center to its boundary. By extension, the radius of a circle or sphere is the length of any such segment. The radius is half the diameter. In science and engineering the term radius of curvature is commonly used as a synonym for radius.
Square	In plane geometry, a square is a polygon with four equal sides, four right angles, and parallel opposite sides. In algebra, the square of a number is that number multiplied by itself.
Perimeter	Perimeter is the distance around a given two-dimensional object. As a general rule, the perimeter of a polygon can always be calculated by adding all the length of the sides together. So, the formula for triangles is P = a + b + c, where a, b and c stand for each side of it. For quadrilaterals the equation is P = a + b + c + d. For equilateral polygons, P = na, where n is the number of sides and a is the side length.
Element	An element or member of a set is an object that when collected together make up the set.
Bisection method	The bisection method is a root-finding algorithm which works by repeatedly dividing an interval in half and then selecting the subinterval in which the root exists.
Elements	In mathematics, the elements, or members of a set or more generally a class are all those objects which when collected together make up the set or class.
Subscript	A subscript is a number, figure, or indicator that appears below the normal line of type, typically used in a formula, mathematical expression, or description of a chemical compound.

Go to **Cram101.com** for the Practice Tests for this Chapter.

Midpoint	midpoint is the middle point of a line segment.
Rate	A rate is a special kind of ratio, indicating a relationship between two measurements with different units, such as miles to gallons or cents to pounds.
Statement	In common philosophical language, a proposition or statement, is the content of an assertion, that is, it is true-or-false and defined by the meaning of a particular piece of language.
Arithmetic	Arithmetic or arithmetics is the oldest and most elementary branch of mathematics, used by almost everyone, for tasks ranging from simple daily counting to advanced science and business calculations.
Composition	In mathematics, a composition of a positive integer n is a way of writing n as a sum of positive integers.

Go to **Cram101.com** for the Practice Tests for this Chapter.
And, **NEVER** highlight a book again!

Secant	Secant is a trigonometric function that is the reciprocal of cosine.
Secant line	secant line of a curve is a line that intersects two or more points on the curve.
Tangent	In trigonometry, the tangent is a function defined as $\tan x = {}^{\sin x}/_{\cos}$ x. The function is so-named because it can be defined as the length of a certain segment of a tangent (in the geometric sense) to the unit circle. In plane geometry, a line is tangent to a curve, at some point, if both line and curve pass through the point with the same direction.
Limiting	limiting Any process by which a specified characteristic usually amplitude of the output of a device is prevented from exceeding a predetermined value.
Slope	Slope is often used to describe the measurement of the steepness, incline, gradient, or grade of a straight line. The slope is defined as the ratio of the "rise" divided by the "run" between two points on a line, or in other words, the ratio of the altitude change to the horizontal distance between any two points on the line.
Tangent line	Tangent line has two distinct but etymologically-related meanings: one in geometry and one in trigonometry.
Measure	A measure is a function that assigns a number to subsets of a given set.
Derivative	The derivative is a measurement of how a function changes when the values of its inputs change.
Differential calculus	Differential calculus, a field in mathematics, is the study of how functions change when their inputs change. The primary object of study in differential calculus is the derivative.
Function	The mathematical concept of a function expresses the intuitive idea of deterministic dependence between two quantities, one of which is viewed as primary and the other as secondary. A function then is a way to associate a unique output for each input of a specified type, for example, a real number or an element of a given set.
Notation	Mathematical notation is used to represent ideas.
Prime	In mathematics, a prime number (or a prime) is a natural number that has exactly two (distinct) natural number divisors, which are 1 and the prime number itself.
Domain	In mathematics, a domain of a k-place relation $L \subseteq X_1$ $\times \ldots \times X_k$ is one of the sets X_j, $1 \le j \le k$. In the special case where k = 2 and $L \subseteq X_1$ class="unicode">$\times X_2$ is a function $L : X_1$ class="unicode">$\to X_2$, it is conventional to refer to X_1 as the domain of the function and to refer to X_2 as the codomain of the function.
Interval	In elementary algebra, an interval is a set that contains every real number between two indicated numbers and may contain the two numbers themselves.
Quotient	In mathematics, a quotient is the end result of a division problem. It can also be expressed as the number of times the divisor divides into the dividend.
Linear	The word linear comes from the Latin word linearis, which means created by lines.
Linear function	A linear function is a first degree polynomial mathematical function of the form: $f(x) = mx + b$ where m and b are real constants and x is a real variable.
Difference quotient	The function difference divided by the point difference is known as the Difference quotient
Subset	A subset is a set whose members are members of another set or a set contained within another

Go to **Cram101.com** for the Practice Tests for this Chapter.
And, **NEVER** highlight a book again!

Numerator	A numerator is a numeral used to indicate a count. The most common use of the word today is to name the part of a fraction that tells the number or count of equal parts.
Square	In plane geometry, a square is a polygon with four equal sides, four right angles, and parallel opposite sides. In algebra, the square of a number is that number multiplied by itself.
Expression	An expression is a combination of numbers, operators, grouping symbols and/or free variables and bound variables arranged in a meaningful way which can be evaluated..
Denominator	A denominator is the part of a fraction that tells how many equal parts make up a whole, and which is used in the name of the fraction: "halves", "thirds", "fourths" or "quarters", "fifths" and so on.
Perpendicular	In geometry, two lines or planes if one falls on the other in such a way as to create congruent adjacent angles. The term may be used as a noun or adjective. Thus, referring to Figure 1, the line AB is the perpendicular to CD through the point B.
Horizontal	In astronomy, geography, geometry and related sciences and contexts, a plane is said to be horizontal at a given point if it is locally perpendicular to the gradient of the gravity field, i.e., with the direction of the gravitational force at that point.
Origin	In mathematics, the origin of a coordinate system is the point where the axes of the system intersect.
Endpoint	In geometry, an endpoint is a point at which a line segment or ray terminates.
Continuous	A continuous function is a function for which, intuitively, small changes in the input result in small changes in the output.
Proof	In mathematics, a proof is a demonstration that, assuming certain axioms, some statement is necessarily true.
Theorem	In mathematics, a theorem is a statement that can be proved on the basis of explicitly stated or previously agreed assumptions.
Graph of a function	In mathematics, the graph of a function f is the collection of all ordered pairs . In particular, graph means the graphical representation of this collection, in the form of a curve or surface, together with axes, etc. Graphing on a Cartesian plane is sometimes referred to as curve sketching.
Real number	In mathematics, a real number may be described informally as a number that can be given by an infinite decimal representation.
Rational	In mathematics, a rational number is a number which can be expressed as a ratio of two integers. Non-integer rational numbers (commonly called fractions) are usually written as the vulgar fraction a / b, where b is not zero.
Irrational	In mathematics, an irrational number is any real number that is not a rational number- that is, it is a number which cannot be expressed as a fraction m/n, where m and n are integers.
Graphs	Graphs are the basic objects of study in graph theory. Informally speaking, a graph is a set of objects called points, nodes, or vertices connected by links called lines or edges.
Trace	In linear algebra, the trace of an n-by-n square matrix A is defined to be the sum of the elements on the main diagonal of A,
Constant	In mathematics and the mathematical sciences, a constant is a fixed, but possibly unspecified, value. This is in contrast to a variable, which is not fixed.
Constant function	Constant function is a function whose values do not vary and thus are constant.

Go to **Cram101.com** for the Practice Tests for this Chapter.

Multiple	A multiple of a number is the product of that number with any integer.
Sum	A sum is the result of the addition of a set of numbers. The numbers may be natural numbers, complex numbers, matrices, or still more complicated objects. An infinite sum is a subtle procedure known as a series.
Identity	An identity is an equality that remains true regardless of the values of any variables that appear within it, to distinguish it from an equality which is true under more particular conditions.
Identity function	An identity function is a function that does not have any effect: it always returns the same value that was used as its argument.
Scalar	In linear algebra, real numbers are called scalars and relate to vectors in a vector space through the operation of scalar multiplication, in which a vector can be multiplied by a number to produce another vector.
Product	In mathematics, a product is the result of multiplying, or an expression that identifies factors to be multiplied.
Product rule	The product rule governs the differentiation of products of differentiable functions.
Hypothesis	A hypothesis consists either of a suggested explanation for a phenomenon or of a reasoned proposal suggesting a possible correlation between multiple phenomena.
Polynomial	In mathematics, a polynomial is an expression that is constructed from one or more variables and constants, using only the operations of addition, subtraction, multiplication, and constant positive whole number exponents. is a polynomial. Note in particular that division by an expression containing a variable is not in general allowed in polynomials. [1]
Multiplication	In mathematics, multiplication is an elementary arithmetic operation. When one of the numbers is a whole number, multiplication is the repeated sum of the other number.
Reciprocal	In mathematics, the multiplicative inverse of a number x, denoted $1/x$ or x^{-1}, is the number which, when multiplied by x, yields 1. The multiplicative inverse of x is also called the reciprocal of x.
Indeterminate form	In calculus and other branches of mathematical analysis, an indeterminate form is an algebraic expression obtained in the context of limits.
Quotient rule	The quotient rule is a method of finding the derivative of a function that is the quotient of two other functions for which derivatives exist.
Minus	The plus and minus signs are mathematical symbols used to represent the notions of positive and negative as well as the operations of addition and subtraction.
Rational function	In mathematics, a rational function is any function which can be written as the ratio of two polynomial functions.
Triangle	A triangle is one of the basic shapes of geometry: a polygon with three vertices and three sides which are straight line segments.
Quadratic function	A quadratic function is a polynomial function of the form $f(x) = ax^2 + bx + c$, where a, b, c are real numbers and a class="unicode"> , 0.
Coefficient	In mathematics, a coefficient is a constant multiplicative factor of a certain object. The object can be such things as a variable, a vector, a function, etc. For example, the coefficient of $9x^2$ is 9.
Curve	In mathematics, the concept of a curve tries to capture the intuitive idea of a geometrical one-dimensional and continuous object. A simple example is the circle.

Go to **Cram101.com** for the Practice Tests for this Chapter.

Units	The units of measurement are a globally standardized and modernized form of the metric system.
Coordinate	A coordinate is a set of numbers that designate location in a given reference system, such as x,y in a planar coordinate system or an x,y,z in a three-dimensional coordinate system.
Axes	An axes is when two lines intersect somewhere on a plane creating a right angle at intersection
Intersection	In mathematics, the intersection of two sets A and B is the set that contains all elements of A that also belong to B (or equivalently, all elements of B that also belong to A), but no other elements.
Inductive	In mathematics, for a statement to be mathematically inductive, such a statement must be true of all natural numbers.
Sine	Sine is a trigonemtric function that is important when studying triangles and modeling periodic phenomena, among other applications.
Cosine	The cosine of an angle is the ratio of the length of the adjacent side to the length of the hypotenuse.
Ratio	A ratio is a quantity that denotes the proportional amount or magnitude of one quantity relative to another.
Engineering	Engineering is the design, analysis, and/or construction of works for practical purposes.
Element	An element or member of a set is an object that when collected together make up the set.
Elements	In mathematics, the elements , or members of a set or more generally a class are all those objects which when collected together make up the set or class.
Leibniz	Leibniz was a German mathematician and philosopher. He invented calculus independently of Newton, and his notation is the one in general use since.
Leibniz notation	Leibniz notation named in honor of the 17th century German philosopher and mathematician Gottfried Wilhelm Leibniz, was originally the use of expressions such as dx and dy and to represent "infinitely small" or infinitesimal increments of quantities x and y, just as Äx and Äy represent finite increments of x and y respectively.
Turn	A turn is 360° or 2ð radians.
Greater than	In mathematics, an inequality is a statement about the relative size or order of two objects. For example 14 > 10, or 14 is greater than 10.
Degree	In mathematics, there are several meanings of degree depending on the subject.
Mathematical induction	Mathematical induction is a method of mathematical proof typically used to establish that a given statement is true of all natural numbers
Conjecture	In mathematics, a conjecture is a mathematical statement which appears likely to be true, but has not been formally proven to be true under the rules of mathematical logic.
Rate	A rate is a special kind of ratio, indicating a relationship between two measurements with different units, such as miles to gallons or cents to pounds.
Power	Power has many meanings, most of which simply .
Binomial Theorem	In mathematics, the binomial theorem is an important formula giving the expansion of powers of sums.
Expansion	An expansion of a product of sums expresses it as a sum of products by using the fact that multiplication distributes over addition.

Go to **Cram101.com** for the Practice Tests for this Chapter.

Binomial	In elementary algebra, a binomial is a polynomial with two terms: the sum of two monomials. It is the simplest kind of polynomial except for a monomial.
Average	In mathematics, an average, mean, or central tendency of a data set refers to a measure of the "middle" or "expected" value of the data set.
Velocity	Velocity of an object is its speed in a particular direction.
Period	In business, particularly accounting, a period is the time intervals that the accounts, statement, payments, or other calculations cover.
Diagram	A diagram is a simplified and structured visual representation of concepts, ideas, constructions, relations, statistical data, anatomy etc used in all aspects of human activities to visualize and clarify the topic.
Acceleration	Acceleration is defined as the rate of change or derivative with respect to time of velocity.
Meter	The metre (or meter, see spelling differences) is a measure of length. It is the basic unit of length in the metric system and in the International System of Units (SI), used around the world for general and scientific purposes.
Mile	A mile is a unit of length, usually used to measure distance, in a number of different systems, including Imperial units, United States customary units and Norwegian/Swedish mil. Its size can vary from system to system, but in each is between 1 and 10 kilometers. In contemporary English contexts mile refers to either:
Miles per hour	Miles per hour is a unit of speed, expressing the number of international miles covered per hour.
Galileo Galilei	Galileo Galilei was an Italian physicist, mathematician, astronomer, and philosopher who is closely associated with the scientific revolution.
Altitude	In geometry, an altitude of a triangle is a straight line through a vertex and perpendicular to (i.e. forming a right angle with) the opposite side or an extension of the opposite side.
Coterminal	Initial objects are also called coterminal, and terminal objects are also called final.
Calculation	A calculation is a deliberate process for transforming one or more inputs into one or more results.
Elevation	The elevation of a geographic location is its height above a fixed reference point, often the mean sea level.
Equator	The equator is an imaginary line on the Earth's surface equidistant from the North Pole and South Pole.
Profit	Profit, from Latin meaning "to make progress", is defined in two different ways. Pure economic profit is the increase in wealth that an investor has from making an investment, taking into consideration all costs associated with that investment including the opportunity cost of capital.
Variable	A variable is a symbolic representation denoting a quantity or expression. It often represents an "unknown" quantity that has the potential to change.
Revenue	Revenue is a business term for the amount of money that a company receives from its activities in a given period, mostly from sales of products and/or services to customers
Nonnegative	The nonnegative integers are all the integers from zero on upwards.
Marginal cost	marginal cost is the change in total cost that arises when the quantity produced changes by one unit.
Marginal revenue	marginal revenue is the extra revenue that an additional unit of product will bring a firm.

Go to **Cram101.com** for the Practice Tests for this Chapter.

It can also be described as the change in total revenue/change in number of units sold.

Component

In mathematics, in the field of group theory, a component of a group is a quasisimple subnormal subgroup.

Circle

In Euclidean geometry, a circle is the set of all points in a plane at a fixed distance, called the radius, from a given point, the center.

Radius

In classical geometry, a radius of a circle or sphere is any line segment from its center to its boundary. By extension, the radius of a circle or sphere is the length of any such segment. The radius is half the diameter. In science and engineering the term radius of curvature is commonly used as a synonym for radius.

Volume

The volume of a solid object is the three-dimensional concept of how much space it occupies, often quantified numerically.

Cube

A cube is a three-dimensional solid object bounded by six square faces, facets, or sides, with three meeting at each vertex.

Diagonal

A diagonal can refer to a line joining two nonadjacent vertices of a polygon or polyhedron, or in some contexts any upward or downward sloping line. .

Sphere

In mathematics, a sphere is the set of all points in three-dimensional space (R^3) which are at distance r from a fixed point of that space, where r is a positive real number called the radius of the sphere. The fixed point is called the center or centre, and is not part of the sphere itself.

Diameter

In geometry, a diameter (Greek words diairo = divide and metro = measure) of a circle is any straight line segment that passes through the centre and whose endpoints are on the circular boundary, or, in more modern usage, the length of such a line segment. When using the word in the more modern sense, one speaks of the diameter rather than a diameter, because all diameters of a circle have the same length. This length is twice the radius. The diameter of a circle is also the longest chord that the circle has.

Circumference

The circumference is the distance around a closed curve. Circumference is a kind of perimeter.

Rectangle

In geometry, a rectangle is defined as a quadrilateral where all four of its angles are right angles.

Sector

A circular sector or circle sector also known as a pie piece is the portion of a circle enclosed by two radii and an arc.

Central

Central is an adjective usually refering to being in the centre.

Radian

The radian is a unit of plane angle. It is represented by the symbol "rad" or, more rarely, by the superscript c (for "circular measure"). For example, an angle of 1.2 radians would be written "1.2 rad" or "1.2c" (second symbol can produce confusion with centigrads).

Cylinder

In mathematics, a cylinder is a quadric surface, with the following equation in Cartesian coordinates: $(x/_a)^2 + (y/_b)^2 = 1$.

Returns

Returns, in economics and political economy, are the distributions or payments awarded to the various suppliers of the factors of production.

Amount

amount is a kind of property which exists as magnitude or multitude. It is among the basic classes of things along with quality, substance, change, and relation.

Chain rule

In calculus, the chain rule is a formula for the derivative of the composite of two functions.

Coordinate

In mathematics and its applications, a coordinate system is a system for assigning an n-tuple

system	of numbers or scalars to each point in an n-dimensional space.
Proofs	Mathematical proofs are demonstrations that,assuming certain axioms, some statement is necessarily true.
Parentheses	Parentheses, either of the curved-bracket punctuation marks that together make a set of parentheses
Check	A check is a negotiable instrument instructing a financial institution to pay a specific amount of a specific currency from a specific demand account held in the maker/depositor face=symbol>¢s name with that institution. Both the maker and payee may be natural persons or legal entities.
Composition	In mathematics, a composition of a positive integer n is a way of writing n as a sum of positive integers.
Argument	In mathematics, science including computer science, linguistics and engineering, an argument is, generally speaking, an independent variable or input to a function.
Force	In physics, force is an influence that may cause an object to accelerate. It may be experienced as a lift, a push, or a pull. The actual acceleration of the body is determined by the vector sum of all forces acting on it, known as net force or resultant force.
Right circular cone	right circular cone is a three-dimensional geometric shape formed by straight lines through a fixed point vertex to the points of a fixed curve directrix.
Cone	A cone is a three-dimensional geometric shape formed by straight lines through a fixed point (vertex) to the points of a fixed curve (directrix)
Triple	In mathematics, a triple is an n-tuple with n being 3.
Multiplicity	The multiplicity of a member of a multiset is how many memberships in the multiset it has.
Factor theorem	The factor theorem is a theorem for finding out the factors of a polynomial.
Equilateral	In geometry, an equilateral polygon is a polygon which has all sides of the same length.
Equilateral triangle	An Equilateral Triangle is a triangle in which all sides are of equal length.
Newton	Sir Isaac Newton, was an English physicist, mathematician, astronomer, natural philosopher, and alchemist, regarded by many as the greatest figure in the history of science
Trigonometric	In mathematics, the trigonometric functions are functions of an angle; they are important when studying triangles and modeling periodic phenomena, among many other applications.
Trigonometric functions	The trigonometric functions are functions of an angle; they are important when studying triangles and modeling periodic phenomena, among many other applications.
Radian measure	radian measure is a unit of plane angle, equal to 180/ð degrees, or about 57.2958 degrees
Pendulum	A pendulum is an object that is attached to a pivot point so that it can swing freely.
Angular	In physics, the angular momentum of an object rotating about some reference point is the measure of the extent to which the object will continue to rotate about that point unless acted upon by an external torque.
Isosceles	An Isosceles triange is a triangle with at least two sides of equal length.
Implicit differentiation	Implicit differentiation is to give an equation R(x,y) = S(x,y) that at least in part has the same graph as y = f(x).
Independent variable	In mathematics, an independent variable is any of the arguments, i.e. "inputs", to a function. Thus if we have a function f(x), then x is a independent variable.

Go to **Cram101.com** for the Practice Tests for this Chapter.

Dependent variable	In a function the dependent variable, is the variable which is the value, i.e. the "output", of the function.
Integers	The integers are the only integral domain whose positive elements are well-ordered, and in which order is preserved by addition. Like the natural numbers, the integers form a countably infinite set. The set of all integers is usually denoted in mathematics by a boldface Z .
Statement	In common philosophical language, a proposition or statement, is the content of an assertion, that is, it is true-or-false and defined by the meaning of a particular piece of language.
General form	One of the three formats applicable to a quadratic function is the general form which is defined as $f = ax^2 + bx + c$.
Center	In geometry, the center of an object is a point in some sense in the middle of the object.
Parabola	In mathematics, the parabola is a conic section generated by the intersection of a right circular conical surface and a plane parallel to a generating straight line of that surface. It can also be defined as locus of points in a plane which are equidistant from a given point.
Curves	In mathematics, curves are the intuitive idea of a geometrical one-dimensional and continuous object.
Orthogonal	In mathematics, orthogonal is synonymous with perpendicular when used as a simple adjective that is not part of any longer phrase with a standard definition. It means at right angles. It comes from the Greek á½€Ï Î¸ÏŒÏ, orthos, meaning "straight", used by Euclid to mean right; and Î³Ï‰Î½Î¯Î± gonia, meaning angle. Two streets that cross each other at a right angle are orthogonal to one another.
Right angle	In geometry and trigonometry, a right angle is defined as an angle between two straight intersecting lines of ninety degrees, or one-quarter of a circle.
Ellipse	In mathematics, an ellipse .
Orthogonal trajectory	In mathematics, a orthogonal trajectory is a family of curves in the plane that intersect a given family of curves at right angles.
Hyperbola	In mathematics, a hyperbola is a type of conic section defined as the intersection between a right circular conical surface and a plane which cuts through both halves of the cone.
Lemniscate	In mathematics, the Lemniscate of Bernoulli is an eight-shaped algebraic curve described by a Cartesian equation
Parametric	Parametric statistics are statistics that estimate population parameters.
Mode	In statistics, mode means the most frequent value assumed by a random variable, or occurring in a sampling of a random variable.
Cissoid	A cissoid is a curve derived from a fixed point O and two other curves á and â. Every line through O cutting á at A and â at B cuts the cissoid at the midpoint of AB.
Unit circle	Unit circle is a circle with a unit radius, i.e., a circle whose radius is 1.
Nautical mile	A nautical mile, sea mile or nautimile is a unit of length. It is accepted for use with the International System of Units (SI), but it is not an SI unit.[1] The nautical mile is used around the world for maritime and aviation purposes. It is commonly used in international law and treaties, especially regarding the limits of territorial waters. It developed from the geographical mile.
Knot	A knot is a method for fastening or securing linear material such as rope by tying or interweaving. It may consist of a length of one or more segments of rope, string, webbing, twine, strap or even chain interwoven so as to create in the line the ability to bind to

Go to **Cram101.com** for the Practice Tests for this Chapter.

itself or to some other object - the "load". Knots have been the subject of interest both for their ancient origins, common use, and the mathematical implications of knot theory.

Opposite	In mathematics, the additive inverse, or opposite of a number n is the number that, when added to n, yields zero. The additive inverse of n is denoted −n. For example, 7 is −7, because 7 + (−7) = 0, and the additive inverse of −0.3 is 0.3, because −0.3 + 0.3 = 0.
Additive inverse	In mathematics, the additive inverse of a number n is the number that, when added to n, yields zero. The additive inverse of n is denoted −n. For example, 7 is −7, because 7 + (−7) = 0, and the additive inverse of −0.3 is 0.3, because −0.3 + 0.3 = 0.
Springs	Springs are flexible, elastic objects used to store mechanical energy.
Orbit	In physics, an orbit is the path that an object makes around another object while under the influence of a source of centripetal force, such as gravity.
Perimeter	Perimeter is the distance around a given two-dimensional object. As a general rule, the perimeter of a polygon can always be calculated by adding all the length of the sides together. So, the formula for triangles is P = a + b + c, where a, b and c stand for each side of it. For quadrilaterals the equation is P = a + b + c + d. For equilateral polygons, P = na, where n is the number of sides and a is the side length.
Minutes	Minutes are a measure of time.
Light	Light is electromagnetic radiation with a wavelength that is visible to the eye (visible light) or, in a technical or scientific context, electromagnetic radiation of any wavelength.
Speed of light	The speed of light in a vacuum is an important physical constant denoted by the letter c for constant or the Latin word celeritas meaning "swiftness
Mass	Mass is the property of a physical object that quantifies the amount of matter and energy it is equivalent to.
Kite	In geometry a kite, or deltoid, is a quadrilateral with two pairs of congruent adjacent sides.
Plane	In mathematics, a plane is a two-dimensional manifold or surface that is perfectly flat.
Angular velocity	In physics, the angular velocity is a vector quantity (more precisely, a pseudovector) which specifies the angular speed at which an object is rotating along with the direction in which it is rotating.
Differential	A differential is traditionally an infinitesimally small change in a variable.
Circular motion	In physics, circular motion is rotation along a circle: a circular path or a circular orbit. The rotation around a fixed axis of a three-dimensional body involves circular motion of its parts. We can talk about circular motion of an object if we ignore its size, so that we have the motion of a point mass in a plane.
Arc	In Euclidean geometry, an arc is a closed segment of a differentiable curve in the two-dimensional plane; for example, a circular arc is a segment of a circle.
Kinetic energy	The kinetic energy of an object is the extra energy which it possesses due to its motion.
Projection	In mathematics, a projection is any one of several different types of functions, mappings, operations, or transformations.
Increment	An increment is an increase, either of some fixed amount, for example added regularly, or of a variable amount.
Root	In mathematics, a root of a complex-valued function f is a member x of the domain of f such that f(x) vanishes at x, that is, x : f (x) = 0.

Proper	A proper fraction is a fraction in which the absolute value of the numerator is less than the denominator--hence, the absolute value of the fraction is less than 1.
Sequence	In mathematics, a sequence is an ordered list of objects. Like a set, it contains members, also called elements or terms, and the number of terms is called the length of the sequence. Unlike a set, order matters, and the exact same elements can appear multiple times at different positions in the sequence.
Concavity	The word concavity means curving in or hollowed inward.
Ring	In mathematics, a ring is an algebraic structure in which addition and multiplication are defined and have properties listed below.
Gallon	U.S. liquid gallon is legally defined as 231 cubic inches, and is equal to 3.785411784 litres or abotu 0.13368 cubic feet. This is the most common definition of a gallon. The U.S. fluid ounce is defined as 1/128 of a U.S. gallon.
Amplitude	The amplitude is a nonnegative scalar measure of a wave's magnitude of oscillation, that is, the magnitude of the maximum disturbance in the medium during one wave cycle.
Temperature	Temperature is a physical property of a system that underlies the common notions of hot and cold; something that is hotter has the greater temperature.
Even function	Even function are functions which satisfy particular symmetry relations, with respect to taking additive inverses.
Algorithm	In mathematics, computing, linguistics, and related disciplines, an algorithm is a finite list of well-defined instructions for accomplishing some task which, given an initial state, will terminate in a defined end-state.
Feature	In geographic information systems, a feature comprises an entity with a geographic location, typically determined by points, arcs, or polygons. Carriageways and cadastres exemplify feature data.
Rational Number	In mathematics, a rational number is a number which can be expressed as a ratio of two integers. Non-integer rational numbers (commonly called fractions) are usually written as the vulgar fraction a / b, where b is not zero.

Go to **Cram101.com** for the Practice Tests for this Chapter.

Continuous	A continuous function is a function for which, intuitively, small changes in the input result in small changes in the output.
Notation	Mathematical notation is used to represent ideas.
Prime	In mathematics, a prime number (or a prime) is a natural number that has exactly two (distinct) natural number divisors, which are 1 and the prime number itself.
Slope	Slope is often used to describe the measurement of the steepness, incline, gradient, or grade of a straight line. The slope is defined as the ratio of the "rise" divided by the "run" between two points on a line, or in other words, the ratio of the altitude change to the horizontal distance between any two points on the line.
Mean	The mean, the average in everyday English, which is also called the arithmetic mean (and is distinguished from the geometric mean or harmonic mean). The average is also called the sample mean. The expected value of a random variable, which is also called the population mean.
Theorem	In mathematics, a theorem is a statement that can be proved on the basis of explicitly stated or previously agreed assumptions.
Derivative	The derivative is a measurement of how a function changes when the values of its inputs change.
Differential calculus	Differential calculus, a field in mathematics, is the study of how functions change when their inputs change. The primary object of study in differential calculus is the derivative.
Interval	In elementary algebra, an interval is a set that contains every real number between two indicated numbers and may contain the two numbers themselves.
Velocity	Velocity of an object is its speed in a particular direction.
Horizontal	In astronomy, geography, geometry and related sciences and contexts, a plane is said to be horizontal at a given point if it is locally perpendicular to the gradient of the gravity field, i.e., with the direction of the gravitational force at that point.
Tangent	In trigonometry, the tangent is a function defined as $\tan x = \sin x /_{\cos}$ x. The function is so-named because it can be defined as the length of a certain segment of a tangent (in the geometric sense) to the unit circle. In plane geometry, a line is tangent to a curve, at some point, if both line and curve pass through the point with the same direction.
Tangent line	Tangent line has two distinct but etymologically-related meanings: one in geometry and one in trigonometry.
Conclusion	In a mathematical proof or a syllogism, a conclusion is a statement that is the logical consequence of preceding statements.
Proof	In mathematics, a proof is a demonstration that, assuming certain axioms, some statement is necessarily true.
Polynomial	In mathematics, a polynomial is an expression that is constructed from one or more variables and constants, using only the operations of addition, subtraction, multiplication, and constant positive whole number exponents. is a polynomial. Note in particular that division by an expression containing a variable is not in general allowed in polynomials. [1]
Function	The mathematical concept of a function expresses the intuitive idea of deterministic dependence between two quantities, one of which is viewed as primary and the other as secondary. A function then is a way to associate a unique output for each input of a specified type, for example, a real number or an element of a given set.

Go to **Cram101.com** for the Practice Tests for this Chapter.

Check	A check is a negotiable instrument instructing a financial institution to pay a specific amount of a specific currency from a specific demand account held in the maker/depositor face=symbol>¢s name with that institution. Both the maker and payee may be natural persons or legal entities.
Root	In mathematics, a root of a complex-valued function f is a member x of the domain of f such that f(x) vanishes at x, that is, x : f (x) = 0.
Consecutive	Consecutive means in succession or back-to-back
Real number	In mathematics, a real number may be described informally as a number that can be given by an infinite decimal representation.
Constant	In mathematics and the mathematical sciences, a constant is a fixed, but possibly unspecified, value. This is in contrast to a variable, which is not fixed.
Acceleration	Acceleration is defined as the rate of change or derivative with respect to time of velocity.
Mile	A mile is a unit of length, usually used to measure distance, in a number of different systems, including Imperial units, United States customary units and Norwegian/Swedish mil. Its size can vary from system to system, but in each is between 1 and 10 kilometers. In contemporary English contexts mile refers to either:
Miles per hour	Miles per hour is a unit of speed, expressing the number of international miles covered per hour.
Minutes	Minutes are a measure of time.
Hypotheses	Hypotheses consists either of a suggested explanation for a phenomenon or of a reasoned proposal suggesting a possible correlation between multiple phenomena.
Graphs	Graphs are the basic objects of study in graph theory. Informally speaking, a graph is a set of objects called points, nodes, or vertices connected by links called lines or edges.
Intercept	Any point where a graph makes contact with an coordinate axis is called an intercept of the graph
Rational	In mathematics, a rational number is a number which can be expressed as a ratio of two integers. Non-integer rational numbers (commonly called fractions) are usually written as the vulgar fraction a / b, where b is not zero.
Irrational	In mathematics, an irrational number is any real number that is not a rational number- that is, it is a number which cannot be expressed as a fraction m/n, where m and n are integers.
Infinite	infinite is the state of being greater than any finite real or natural number, however large.
Endpoint	In geometry, an endpoint is a point at which a line segment or ray terminates.
Domain	In mathematics, a domain of a k-place relation L $\subseteq$ X_1 × ... × X_k is one of the sets X_j, $1 \le j \le k$. In the special case where k = 2 and L $\subseteq$ X_1 class="unicode">× X_2 is a function L : X_1 class="unicode">→ X_2, it is conventional to refer to X_1 as the domain of the function and to refer to X_2 as the codomain of the function.
Discontinuity	Continuous functions are of utmost importance in mathematics and applications. However, not all functions are continuous. If a function is not continuous at a point in its domain, one says that it has a discontinuity there. The set of all points of discontinuity of a function may be a discrete set, a dense set, or even the entire domain of the function.
Curve	In mathematics, the concept of a curve tries to capture the intuitive idea of a geometrical

one-dimensional and continuous object. A simple example is the circle.

Curves	In mathematics, curves are the intuitive idea of a geometrical one-dimensional and continuous object.
Continuous function	A continuous function is a function for which, intuitively, small changes in the input result in small changes in the output.
Converse	Converse Logic is a concept in traditional logic referring to a "type of immediate inference in which from a given proposition another proposition is inferred which has as its subject the predicate of the original proposition and as its predicate the subject of the original proposition (the quality of the proposition being retained)."
Implication	In logic and mathematics, logical implication is a logical relation that holds between a set T of formulas and a formula B when every model (or interpretation or valuation) of T is also a model of B.
Potential	In physics, a potential may refer to the scalar potential or to the vector potential.
Physics	Physics, Greek for "knowledge of nature," is the branch of science concerned with the discovery and characterization of universal laws which govern matter, energy, space, and time.
Kinetic energy	The kinetic energy of an object is the extra energy which it possesses due to its motion.
Law of Conservation of Energy	In physics, the law of conservation of energy states that the total amount of energy in an isolated system remains constant, although it may change forms, e.g. friction turns kinetic energy into thermal energy.
Expression	An expression is a combination of numbers, operators, grouping symbols and/or free variables and bound variables arranged in a meaningful way which can be evaluated..
Equivalent	Equivalence is the condition of being equivalent or essentially equal.
Meter	The metre (or meter, see spelling differences) is a measure of length. It is the basic unit of length in the metric system and in the International System of Units (SI), used around the world for general and scientific purposes.
Method for finding	The easiest method for finding prime numbers resides in the use of the Sieve of Eratosthenes, an algorithm that discovers all prime numbers to a specified integer.
Engineering	Engineering is the design, analysis, and/or construction of works for practical purposes.
Extreme value	The term extreme value refers to the largest and the smallest element of a set.
Local maximum	A real-valued function f defined on the real line is said to have a Local maximum point at the point x , if there exists some $\varepsilon > 0$, such that f when $x - x < \varepsilon$.
Maxima	Maxima is a free computer algebra system based on a 1982 version of Macsyma
Maxima and minima	Maxima and minima are points in the domain of a function at which the function takes a largest value or smallest value, either within a given neighborhood or on the function domain in its entirety.
Minima	In mathematics, maxima and minima, known collectively as extrema, are points in the domain of a function at which the function takes a largest value .
Critical point	Critical point is a point on the domain of a function
Parabola	In mathematics, the parabola is a conic section generated by the intersection of a right circular conical surface and a plane parallel to a generating straight line of that surface. It can also be defined as locus of points in a plane which are equidistant from a given point.

Test	Acid test ratio measures the ability of a company to use its near cash or quick assets to immediately extinguish its current liabilities.
Determining	Determining the expected value of a random variable displays the average or central value of the variable.It is a summary value of the distribution of the variable.
Direct	In mathematics and logic, a direct proof is a way of showing the truth or falsehood of a given statement by a straightforward combination of established facts, usually existing lemmas and theorems, without making any further assumptions.
Hypothesis	A hypothesis consists either of a suggested explanation for a phenomenon or of a reasoned proposal suggesting a possible correlation between multiple phenomena.
Sine	Sine is a trigonemtric function that is important when studying triangles and modeling periodic phenomena, among other applications.
Profit	Profit, from Latin meaning "to make progress", is defined in two different ways. Pure economic profit is the increase in wealth that an investor has from making an investment, taking into consideration all costs associated with that investment including the opportunity cost of capital.
Marginal cost	marginal cost is the change in total cost that arises when the quantity produced changes by one unit.
Marginal revenue	marginal revenue is the extra revenue that an additional unit of product will bring a firm. It can also be described as the change in total revenue/change in number of units sold.
Revenue	Revenue is a business term for the amount of money that a company receives from its activities in a given period, mostly from sales of products and/or services to customers
Newton	Sir Isaac Newton, was an English physicist, mathematician, astronomer, natural philosopher, and alchemist, regarded by many as the greatest figure in the history of science
Reasoning	Deductive reasoning is the kind of reasoning in which the conclusion is necessitated by, or reached from, previously known facts (the premises).
Bounded	In mathematical analysis and related areas of mathematics, a set is called bounded, if it is, in a certain sense, of finite size.
Extrema	in mathematics, maxima and minima, known collectively as extrema, are the largest value maximum or smallest value minimum, that a function takes in a point either within a given neighborhood or on the function domain in its entirety global extremum.
Negative number	A negative number is a number that is less than zero.
Exponentiating	Exponentiating is a mathematical operation, written a^n, involving two numbers, the base a and the exponent n.
Exponentiation	Exponentiation is a mathematical operation, written a^n, involving two numbers, the base a and the exponent n.
Rational Number	In mathematics, a rational number is a number which can be expressed as a ratio of two integers. Non-integer rational numbers (commonly called fractions) are usually written as the vulgar fraction a / b, where b is not zero.
Coefficient	In mathematics, a coefficient is a constant multiplicative factor of a certain object. The object can be such things as a variable, a vector, a function, etc. For example, the coefficient of $9x^2$ is 9.
Harmonic	In acoustics and telecommunication, the harmonic of a wave is a component frequency of the signal that is an integer multiple of the fundamental frequency.

Go to **Cram101.com** for the Practice Tests for this Chapter.

Harmonic motion	Simple harmonic motion is the motion of a simple harmonic oscillator, a motion that is neither driven nor damped. Complex harmonic motion is the superposition — linear combination — of several simultaneous simple harmonic motions.
Cube	A cube is a three-dimensional solid object bounded by six square faces, facets, or sides, with three meeting at each vertex.
Cubes	Cubes are of a number n in its third power-the result of multiplying it by itself three times.
Sum	A sum is the result of the addition of a set of numbers. The numbers may be natural numbers, complex numbers, matrices, or still more complicated objects. An infinite sum is a subtle procedure known as a series.
Projectile	A projectile is any object propelled through space by the applicationp of a force.
Elevation	The elevation of a geographic location is its height above a fixed reference point, often the mean sea level.
Range	In mathematics, the range of a function is the set of all "output" values produced by that function. Given a function f :A $\rightarrow$ B, the range of class="unicode">f, is defined to be the set {x class="unicode"> B:x= class="unicode">f(a) for some a class="unicode"> A}.
Triangle	A triangle is one of the basic shapes of geometry: a polygon with three vertices and three sides which are straight line segments.
Square	In plane geometry, a square is a polygon with four equal sides, four right angles, and parallel opposite sides. In algebra, the square of a number is that number multiplied by itself.
Equilateral	In geometry, an equilateral polygon is a polygon which has all sides of the same length.
Equilateral triangle	An Equilateral Triangle is a triangle in which all sides are of equal length.
Conjunction	In logic and mathematics, logical conjunction (usual symbol and) is a two-place logical operation that results in a value of true if both of its operands are true, otherwise a value of false.
Variable	A variable is a symbolic representation denoting a quantity or expression. It often represents an "unknown" quantity that has the potential to change.
Units	The units of measurement are a globally standardized and modernized form of the metric system.
Isosceles	An Isosceles triange is a triangle with at least two sides of equal length.
Rectangle	In geometry, a rectangle is defined as a quadrilateral where all four of its angles are right angles.
Coordinate	A coordinate is a set of numbers that designate location in a given reference system, such as x,y in a planar coordinate system or an x,y,z in a three-dimensional coordinate system.
Coordinate system	In mathematics and its applications, a coordinate system is a system for assigning an n-tuple of numbers or scalars to each point in an n-dimensional space.
Product	In mathematics, a product is the result of multiplying, or an expression that identifies factors to be multiplied.

Volume	The volume of a solid object is the three-dimensional concept of how much space it occupies, often quantified numerically.
Radius	In classical geometry, a radius of a circle or sphere is any line segment from its center to its boundary. By extension, the radius of a circle or sphere is the length of any such segment. The radius is half the diameter. In science and engineering the term radius of curvature is commonly used as a synonym for radius.
Cylinder	In mathematics, a cylinder is a quadric surface, with the following equation in Cartesian coordinates: $(x/_a)^2 + (y/_b)^2 = 1$.
Lateral	A lateral surface is the surface or face of a solid on its sides. It can also be defined as any face or surface that is not a base.
Amount	amount is a kind of property which exists as magnitude or multitude. It is among the basic classes of things along with quality, substance, change, and relation.
Light	Light is electromagnetic radiation with a wavelength that is visible to the eye (visible light) or, in a technical or scientific context, electromagnetic radiation of any wavelength.
Perimeter	Perimeter is the distance around a given two-dimensional object. As a general rule, the perimeter of a polygon can always be calculated by adding all the length of the sides together. So, the formula for triangles is $P = a + b + c$, where a, b and c stand for each side of it. For quadrilaterals the equation is $P = a + b + c + d$. For equilateral polygons, $P = na$, where n is the number of sides and a is the side length.
Quadratic formula	A quadratic equation with real solutions, called roots, which may be real or complex, is given by the quadratic formula: $x = \frac{-b \pm \sqrt{b^2 - 4ac}}{2a}$.
Reflection	In mathematics, a reflection (also spelled reflexion) is a map that transforms an object into its mirror image.
Experiment	In the scientific method, an experiment (Latin: ex-+-periri, "of (or from) trying"), is a set of actions and observations, performed in the context of solving a particular problem or question, in order to support or falsify a hypothesis or research concerning phenomena.
Incidence	In geometry, the relations of incidence are those such as 'lies on' between points and lines (as in 'point P lies on line L'), and 'intersects face=symbol>¢ (as in 'line L_1 intersects line L_2', in three-dimensional space). That is, they are the binary relations describing how subsets meet.
Travel	Travel is the transport of people on a trip/journey or the process or time involved in a person or object moving from one location to another.
Calculus	Calculus is a mathematical subject that includes the study of limits, derivatives, integrals, and power series and constitutes a major part of modern university curriculum.
Union	In set theory and other branches of mathematics, the union of a collection of sets is the set that contains everything that belongs to any of the sets, but nothing else.
Integers	The integers are the only integral domain whose positive elements are well-ordered, and in which order is preserved by addition. Like the natural numbers, the integers form a countably infinite set. The set of all integers is usually denoted in mathematics by a boldface Z .
Finite	In mathematics, a set is called finite if there is a bijection between the set and some set

Go to Cram101.com for the Practice Tests for this Chapter.

of the form {1, 2, ..., n} where n is a natural number.

Discrete	The word discrete comes from the 15th Century Latin word discretus which means separate.
Manufacturing	Manufacturing is the application of tools and a processing medium to the transformation of raw materials into finished goods for sale.
Capacity	Capacity is the ability to hold, receive or absorb, or a measure thereof, similar to the concept of volume.
Principle	A principle signifies a point or points of probability on a subject e.g., the principle of creativity, which allows for the formation of rule or norm or law by interpretation of the phenomena events that can be created.
Demand	In economics, supply and demand describe market relations between prospective sellers and buyers of a good.
Calculation	A calculation is a deliberate process for transforming one or more inputs into one or more results.
Vertex	In geometry, a vertex is a special kind of point, usually a corner of a polygon, polyhedron, or higher dimensional polytope. In the geometry of curves a vertex is a point of where the first derivative of curvature is zero. In graph theory, a vertex is the fundamental unit out of which graphs are formed
Circle	In Euclidean geometry, a circle is the set of all points in a plane at a fixed distance, called the radius, from a given point, the center.
Space	Space is a set, with some particular properties and usually some additional structure, such as the operations of addition or multiplication, for instance.
Linear	The word linear comes from the Latin word linearis, which means created by lines.
Axes	An axes is when two lines intersect somewhere on a plane creating a right angle at intersection
Pentagon	In geometry, a pentagon is any five-sided polygon.
Carrying capacity	Carrying capacity usually refers to the biological carrying capacity of a population level that can be supported for an organism, given the quantity of food, habitat, water and other life infrastructure present.
Segment	In geometry, a line segment is a part of a line that is bounded by two end points, and contains every point on the line between its end points.
Origin	In mathematics, the origin of a coordinate system is the point where the axes of the system intersect.
Line segment	A line segment is a part of a line that is bounded by two end points, and contains every point on the line between its end points.
Right angle	In geometry and trigonometry, a right angle is defined as an angle between two straight intersecting lines of ninety degrees, or one-quarter of a circle.
Center	In geometry, the center of an object is a point in some sense in the middle of the object.
Right circular cone	right circular cone is a three-dimensional geometric shape formed by straight lines through a fixed point vertex to the points of a fixed curve directrix.
Cone	A cone is a three-dimensional geometric shape formed by straight lines through a fixed point (vertex) to the points of a fixed curve (directrix)
Congruent	In geometry, two sets are called congruent if one can be transformed into the other by an

Go to **Cram101.com** for the Practice Tests for this Chapter.

isometry, i.e., a combination of translations, rotations and reflections.

Plane	In mathematics, a plane is a two-dimensional manifold or surface that is perfectly flat.
Force	In physics, force is an influence that may cause an object to accelerate. It may be experienced as a lift, a push, or a pull. The actual acceleration of the body is determined by the vector sum of all forces acting on it, known as net force or resultant force.
Magnitude	The magnitude of a mathematical object is its size: a property by which it can be larger or smaller than other objects of the same kind; in technical terms, an ordering of the class of objects to which it belongs.
Sphere	In mathematics, a sphere is the set of all points in three-dimensional space (R^3) which are at distance r from a fixed point of that space, where r is a positive real number called the radius of the sphere. The fixed point is called the center or centre, and is not part of the sphere itself.
Kilometer	A kilometer is a unit of length in the metric system, equal to one thousand metres, the current SI base unit of length
Power	Power has many meanings, most of which simply .
Perpendicular	In geometry, two lines or planes if one falls on the other in such a way as to create congruent adjacent angles. The term may be used as a noun or adjective. Thus, referring to Figure 1, the line AB is the perpendicular to CD through the point B.
Mountain	A mountain is a landform that extends above the surrounding terrain in a limited area. A mountain is generally steeper than a hill, but there is no universally accepted standard definition for the height of a mountain or a hill although a mountain usually has an identifiable summit.
Friction	Friction is the force that opposes the relative motion or tendency toward such motion of two surfaces in contact.
Inclined plane	The inclined plane is one of the classical simple machines; as the name suggests, it is a flat surface whose endpoints are at different heights. By moving an object up an inclined plane rather than directly from one height to another, the amount of force required is reduced, at the expense of increasing the distance the object must travel. The mechanical advantage of an inclined plane is the ratio of the length of the sloped surface to the height it spans; this may also be expressed as the cosecant of the angle between the plane and the horizontal.
Net	In topology and related areas of mathematics a net or Moore-Smith sequence is a generalization of a sequence, intended to unify the various notions of limit and generalize them to arbitrary topological spaces.
Net profit	Net profit is an accounting term which is commonly used in business.
Average	In mathematics, an average, mean, or central tendency of a data set refers to a measure of the "middle" or "expected" value of the data set.
Projectile motion	Projectile motion is the path a moving object follows through space.
Coterminal	Initial objects are also called coterminal, and terminal objects are also called final.
Rate	A rate is a special kind of ratio, indicating a relationship between two measurements with different units, such as miles to gallons or cents to pounds.
Gallon	U.S. liquid gallon is legally defined as 231 cubic inches, and is equal to 3.785411784 litres or abotu 0.13368 cubic feet. This is the most common definition of a gallon. The U.S. fluid

ounce is defined as 1/128 of a U.S. gallon.

Trace	In linear algebra, the trace of an n-by-n square matrix A is defined to be the sum of the elements on the main diagonal of A,
Ellipse	In mathematics, an ellipse .
Explanation	The deductive-nomological model is a formalized view of scientific explanation in natural language.
Graph of a function	In mathematics, the graph of a function f is the collection of all ordered pairs . In particular, graph means the graphical representation of this collection, in the form of a curve or surface, together with axes, etc. Graphing on a Cartesian plane is sometimes referred to as curve sketching.
Concavity	The word concavity means curving in or hollowed inward.
Quadratic function	A quadratic function is a polynomial function of the form $f(x) = ax^2 + bx + c$, where a, b, c are real numbers and a class="unicode"> , 0.
Opposite	In mathematics, the additive inverse, or opposite of a number n is the number that, when added to n, yields zero. The additive inverse of n is denoted −n. For example, 7 is −7, because 7 + (−7) = 0, and the additive inverse of −0.3 is 0.3, because −0.3 + 0.3 = 0.
Additive inverse	In mathematics, the additive inverse of a number n is the number that, when added to n, yields zero. The additive inverse of n is denoted −n. For example, 7 is −7, because 7 + (−7) = 0, and the additive inverse of −0.3 is 0.3, because −0.3 + 0.3 = 0.
Arc	In Euclidean geometry, an arc is a closed segment of a differentiable curve in the two-dimensional plane; for example, a circular arc is a segment of a circle.
Even function	Even function are functions which satisfy particular symmetry relations, with respect to taking additive inverses.
Midpoint	midpoint is the middle point of a line segment.
Degree	In mathematics, there are several meanings of degree depending on the subject.
Asymptote	An asymptote is a straight line or curve A to which another curve B approaches closer and closer as one moves along it. As one moves along B, the space between it and the asymptote A becomes smaller and smaller, and can in fact be made as small as one could wish by going far enough along. A curve may or may not touch or cross its asymptote. In fact, the curve may intersect the asymptote an infinite number of times.
Vertical asymptote	Vertical asymptote is a straight line or curve A to which another curve B the one being studied approaches closer and closer as one moves along it.
Rational function	In mathematics, a rational function is any function which can be written as the ratio of two polynomial functions.
Oblique	In geometry, an oblique angle is an angle that is not a 90 degree angle, or an angle that is divisible by 90: 180, 270, 360/0
Symmetry	Symmetry means "constancy", i.e. if something retains a certain feature even after we change a way of looking at it, then it is symmetric.
Period	In business, particularly accounting, a period is the time intervals that the accounts, statement, payments, or other calculations cover.
Extreme point	An extreme point or an extremal point is a point that belongs to the extremity of something.
Interest	Interest is the fee paid on borrowed money.

Go to **Cram101.com** for the Practice Tests for this Chapter.

Proper	A proper fraction is a fraction in which the absolute value of the numerator is less than the denominator--hence, the absolute value of the fraction is less than 1.
Curve sketching	Graphing on a Cartesian plane is sometimes referred to as curve sketching.
Periodic function	A periodic function is a function that repeats its values after some definite period has been added to its independent variable.
Scale	In Euclidean geometry, a uniform scale is a linear transformation that enlargers or diminishes objects, and whose scale factor is the same in all directions. This is also called homothethy.
Hyperbola	In mathematics, a hyperbola is a type of conic section defined as the intersection between a right circular conical surface and a plane which cuts through both halves of the cone.
Number line	A number line is a one-dimensional picture in which the integers are shown as specially-marked points evenly spaced on a line.
Solution set	A solution set is a set of possible values that a variable can take on in order to satisfy a given set of conditions, which may include equations and inequalities.
Implicit differentiation	Implicit differentiation is to give an equation $R(x,y) = S(x,y)$ that at least in part has the same graph as $y = f(x)$.
Differential	A differential is traditionally an infinitesimally small change in a variable.
Proportional	In mathematics, two quantities are called proportional if they vary in such a way that one of the quantities is a constant multiple of the other, or equivalently if they have a constant ratio.
Rocket	A rocket is a vehicle, missile or aircraft which obtains thrust by the reaction to the ejection of fast moving fluid from within a rocket engine.
Right triangle	Right triangle has one 90° internal angle a right angle.

Go to **Cram101.com** for the Practice Tests for this Chapter.

Rectangle	In geometry, a rectangle is defined as a quadrilateral where all four of its angles are right angles.
Inequality	In mathematics, an inequality is a statement about the relative size or order of two objects.
Sum	A sum is the result of the addition of a set of numbers. The numbers may be natural numbers, complex numbers, matrices, or still more complicated objects. An infinite sum is a subtle procedure known as a series.
Greater than	In mathematics, an inequality is a statement about the relative size or order of two objects. For example 14 > 10, or 14 is greater than 10.
Continuous	A continuous function is a function for which, intuitively, small changes in the input result in small changes in the output.
Turn	A turn is 360° or 2ð radians.
Period	In business, particularly accounting, a period is the time intervals that the accounts, statement, payments, or other calculations cover.
Constant	In mathematics and the mathematical sciences, a constant is a fixed, but possibly unspecified, value. This is in contrast to a variable, which is not fixed.
Finite	In mathematics, a set is called finite if there is a bijection between the set and some set of the form $\{1, 2, ..., n\}$ where n is a natural number.
Interval	In elementary algebra, an interval is a set that contains every real number between two indicated numbers and may contain the two numbers themselves.
Units	The units of measurement are a globally standardized and modernized form of the metric system.
Function	The mathematical concept of a function expresses the intuitive idea of deterministic dependence between two quantities, one of which is viewed as primary and the other as secondary. A function then is a way to associate a unique output for each input of a specified type, for example, a real number or an element of a given set.
Continuous function	A continuous function is a function for which, intuitively, small changes in the input result in small changes in the output.
Definite integral	definite integral is an extension of the concept of a sum.
Integral	The integral of a function is an extension of the concept of a sum, and are identified or found through the use of integration.
Integration	Integration is a process of combining or accumulating. It may also refer to:
Subset	A subset is a set whose members are members of another set or a set contained within another
Mean	The mean, the average in everyday English, which is also called the arithmetic mean (and is distinguished from the geometric mean or harmonic mean). The average is also called the sample mean. The expected value of a random variable, which is also called the population mean.
Partition	Generally, a partition is a splitting of something into parts.
Endpoint	In geometry, an endpoint is a point at which a line segment or ray terminates.
Check	A check is a negotiable instrument instructing a financial institution to pay a specific amount of a specific currency from a specific demand account held in the maker/depositor face=symbol>¢s name with that institution. Both the maker and payee may be natural persons or legal entities.

Go to **Cram101.com** for the Practice Tests for this Chapter.

Leibniz	Leibniz was a German mathematician and philosopher. He invented calculus independently of Newton, and his notation is the one in general use since.
Integrand	Integrand is a function that extends the concept of an ordinary sum
Variable	A variable is a symbolic representation denoting a quantity or expression. It often represents an "unknown" quantity that has the potential to change.
Expression	An expression is a combination of numbers, operators, grouping symbols and/or free variables and bound variables arranged in a meaningful way which can be evaluated..
Nonnegative	The nonnegative integers are all the integers from zero on upwards.
Riemann sum	Riemann sum is a method for approximating the values of integrals.
Symbols	Symbols are objects, characters, or other concrete representations of ideas, concepts, or other abstractions.
Curve	In mathematics, the concept of a curve tries to capture the intuitive idea of a geometrical one-dimensional and continuous object. A simple example is the circle.
Determining	Determining the expected value of a random variable displays the average or central value of the variable.It is a summary value of the distribution of the variable.
Bounded	In mathematical analysis and related areas of mathematics, a set is called bounded, if it is, in a certain sense, of finite size.
Discontinuity	Continuous functions are of utmost importance in mathematics and applications. However, not all functions are continuous. If a function is not continuous at a point in its domain, one says that it has a discontinuity there. The set of all points of discontinuity of a function may be a discrete set, a dense set, or even the entire domain of the function.
Regular	In mathematics, a regular function in the sense of algebraic geometry is an everywhere-defined, polynomial function on an algebraic variety V with values in the field K over which V is defined.
Integers	The integers are the only integral domain whose positive elements are well-ordered, and in which order is preserved by addition. Like the natural numbers, the integers form a countably infinite set. The set of all integers is usually denoted in mathematics by a boldface Z .
Mathematical induction	Mathematical induction is a method of mathematical proof typically used to establish that a given statement is true of all natural numbers
Square	In plane geometry, a square is a polygon with four equal sides, four right angles, and parallel opposite sides. In algebra, the square of a number is that number multiplied by itself.
Piecewise	A piecewise defined function $f(x)$ of a real variable x is a function whose definition is given differently on disjoint subsets of its domain.
Finite set	In mathematics, a finite set occurs if there is a bijection between the set and some set of the form 1, 2, ..., n where n is a natural number.
Midpoint	midpoint is the middle point of a line segment.
Theorem	In mathematics, a theorem is a statement that can be proved on the basis of explicitly stated or previously agreed assumptions.
Calculus	Calculus is a mathematical subject that includes the study of limits, derivatives, integrals, and power series and constitutes a major part of modern university curriculum.
Fundamental theorem	In number theory, the fundamental theorem of arithmetic (or unique factorization theorem) states that every natural number greater than 1 can be written as a unique product of prime

numbers.

Additive	In mathematics, the additive inverse, or opposite, of a number n is the number that, when added to n, yields zero. The additive inverse of n is denoted −n.
Proof	In mathematics, a proof is a demonstration that, assuming certain axioms, some statement is necessarily true.
Derivative	The derivative is a measurement of how a function changes when the values of its inputs change.
Real number	In mathematics, a real number may be described informally as a number that can be given by an infinite decimal representation.
Slope	Slope is often used to describe the measurement of the steepness, incline, gradient, or grade of a straight line. The slope is defined as the ratio of the "rise" divided by the "run" between two points on a line, or in other words, the ratio of the altitude change to the horizontal distance between any two points on the line.
Asymptote	An asymptote is a straight line or curve A to which another curve B approaches closer and closer as one moves along it. As one moves along B, the space between it and the asymptote A becomes smaller and smaller, and can in fact be made as small as one could wish by going far enough along. A curve may or may not touch or cross its asymptote. In fact, the curve may intersect the asymptote an infinite number of times.
Origin	In mathematics, the origin of a coordinate system is the point where the axes of the system intersect.
Horizontal	In astronomy, geography, geometry and related sciences and contexts, a plane is said to be horizontal at a given point if it is locally perpendicular to the gradient of the gravity field, i.e., with the direction of the gravitational force at that point.
Concavity	The word concavity means curving in or hollowed inward.
Product	In mathematics, a product is the result of multiplying, or an expression that identifies factors to be multiplied.
Quotient	In mathematics, a quotient is the end result of a division problem. It can also be expressed as the number of times the divisor divides into the dividend.
Symmetry	Symmetry means "constancy", i.e. if something retains a certain feature even after we change a way of looking at it, then it is symmetric.
Composition	In mathematics, a composition of a positive integer n is a way of writing n as a sum of positive integers.
Antiderivative	An antiderivative of a function f is a function F whose derivative is equal to f, i.e., $F' = f$.
Notation	Mathematical notation is used to represent ideas.
Rational	In mathematics, a rational number is a number which can be expressed as a ratio of two integers. Non-integer rational numbers (commonly called fractions) are usually written as the vulgar fraction a / b, where b is not zero.
Differential calculus	Differential calculus, a field in mathematics, is the study of how functions change when their inputs change. The primary object of study in differential calculus is the derivative.
Antidifferen-iation	Antidifferentiation in calculus is primitive or indefinite integral of a function f is a function F whose derivative is equal to f, i.e., F Œ = f. The process of solving for antiderivatives is antidifferentiation

Combination	In combinatorial mathematics, a combination is an un-ordered collection of unique elements.
Linear	The word linear comes from the Latin word linearis, which means created by lines.
Valid	In statistics, a valid measure is one which is measuring what is supposed to measure.
Calculation	A calculation is a deliberate process for transforming one or more inputs into one or more results.
Harmonic	In acoustics and telecommunication, the harmonic of a wave is a component frequency of the signal that is an integer multiple of the fundamental frequency.
Harmonic motion	Simple harmonic motion is the motion of a simple harmonic oscillator, a motion that is neither driven nor damped. Complex harmonic motion is the superposition — linear combination — of several simultaneous simple harmonic motions.
Equilibrium	In economics, economic equilibrium is simply a state of the world where economic forces are balanced and in the absence of external influences the values of economic variables will not change.
Graphs	Graphs are the basic objects of study in graph theory. Informally speaking, a graph is a set of objects called points, nodes, or vertices connected by links called lines or edges.
Curves	In mathematics, curves are the intuitive idea of a geometrical one-dimensional and continuous object.
Congruent	In geometry, two sets are called congruent if one can be transformed into the other by an isometry, i.e., a combination of translations, rotations and reflections.
Fundamental Theorem of Calculus	Fundamental Theorem of Calculus of calculus is the statement that the two central operations of calculus, differentiation and integration, are inverse operations: if a continuous function is first integrated and then differentiated, the original function is retrieved.
Interest	Interest is the fee paid on borrowed money.
Constant of integration	In calculus, the indefinite integral of a given function i.e. the set of all antiderivatives of the function is always written with a constant, the constant of integration.
Coterminal	Initial objects are also called coterminal, and terminal objects are also called final.
Coordinate	A coordinate is a set of numbers that designate location in a given reference system, such as x,y in a planar coordinate system or an x,y,z in a three-dimensional coordinate system.
Velocity	Velocity of an object is its speed in a particular direction.
Absolute value	In mathematics, the absolute value (or modulus) of a real number is its numerical value without regard to its sign.
Acceleration	Acceleration is defined as the rate of change or derivative with respect to time of velocity.
Rate	A rate is a special kind of ratio, indicating a relationship between two measurements with different units, such as miles to gallons or cents to pounds.
Travel	Travel is the transport of people on a trip/journey or the process or time involved in a person or object moving from one location to another.
Galileo Galilei	Galileo Galilei was an Italian physicist, mathematician, astronomer, and philosopher who is closely associated with the scientific revolution.
Mile	A mile is a unit of length, usually used to measure distance, in a number of different systems, including Imperial units, United States customary units and Norwegian/Swedish mil. Its size can vary from system to system, but in each is between 1 and 10 kilometers. In contemporary English contexts mile refers to either:

Go to **Cram101.com** for the Practice Tests for this Chapter.

Plane	In mathematics, a plane is a two-dimensional manifold or surface that is perfectly flat.
Minutes	Minutes are a measure of time.
Chain rule	In calculus, the chain rule is a formula for the derivative of the composite of two functions.
Power	Power has many meanings, most of which simply .
Differential	A differential is traditionally an infinitesimally small change in a variable.
Sine	Sine is a trigonemtric function that is important when studying triangles and modeling periodic phenomena, among other applications.
Solution set	A solution set is a set of possible values that a variable can take on in order to satisfy a given set of conditions, which may include equations and inequalities.
Proper	A proper fraction is a fraction in which the absolute value of the numerator is less than the denominator--hence, the absolute value of the fraction is less than 1.
Circle	In Euclidean geometry, a circle is the set of all points in a plane at a fixed distance, called the radius, from a given point, the center.
Radius	In classical geometry, a radius of a circle or sphere is any line segment from its center to its boundary. By extension, the radius of a circle or sphere is the length of any such segment. The radius is half the diameter. In science and engineering the term radius of curvature is commonly used as a synonym for radius.
Quadrant	A Quadrant consists of one quarter of the coordinate plane.
Ellipse	In mathematics, an ellipse .
Pairs	In mathematics, the conjugate pairs or adjoint matrix of an m-by-n matrix A with complex entries is the n-by-m matrix A* obtained from A by taking the transpose and then taking the complex conjugate of each entry.
Equivalent	Equivalence is the condition of being equivalent or essentially equal.
Domain	In mathematics, a domain of a k-place relation L $\subseteq$ X_1 × ... × X_k is one of the sets X_i, $1 \le j \le k$. In the special case where k = 2 and L $\subseteq$ X_1 class="unicode">× X_2 is a function L : X_1 class="unicode">→ X_2, it is conventional to refer to X_1 as the domain of the function and to refer to X_2 as the codomain of the function.
Average	In mathematics, an average, mean, or central tendency of a data set refers to a measure of the "middle" or "expected" value of the data set.
Trace	In linear algebra, the trace of an n-by-n square matrix A is defined to be the sum of the elements on the main diagonal of A,
Even function	Even function are functions which satisfy particular symmetry relations, with respect to taking additive inverses.
Identity	An identity is an equality that remains true regardless of the values of any variables that appear within it, to distinguish it from an equality which is true under more particular conditions.
Mass	Mass is the property of a physical object that quantifies the amount of matter and energy it is equivalent to.
Density	Density is mass m per unit volume V.

Center	In geometry, the center of an object is a point in some sense in the middle of the object.
Center of mass	In physics, the center of mass of a system of particles is a specific point at which, for many purposes, the system's mass behaves as if it were concentrated.
Projectile	A projectile is any object propelled through space by the applicationp of a force.
Parabola	In mathematics, the parabola is a conic section generated by the intersection of a right circular conical surface and a plane parallel to a generating straight line of that surface. It can also be defined as locus of points in a plane which are equidistant from a given point.
Range	In mathematics, the range of a function is the set of all "output" values produced by that function. Given a function f :A $\rightarrow$ B, the range of class="unicode">f, is defined to be the set {x class="unicode"> B:x= class="unicode">f(a) for some a class="unicode"> A}.
Kilogram	The kilogram or kilogramme is the SI base unit of mass. It is defined as being equal to the mass of the international prototype of the kilogram.
Meter	The metre (or meter, see spelling differences) is a measure of length. It is the basic unit of length in the metric system and in the International System of Units (SI), used around the world for general and scientific purposes.
Square root	In mathematics, a square root of a number x is a number r such that r^2 = x, or in words, a number r whose square (the result of multiplying the number by itself) is x.
Root	In mathematics, a root of a complex-valued function f is a member x of the domain of f such that f(x) vanishes at x, that is, x : f (x) = 0.
Arithmetic	Arithmetic or arithmetics is the oldest and most elementary branch of mathematics, used by almost everyone, for tasks ranging from simple daily counting to advanced science and business calculations.
Coordinate system	In mathematics and its applications, a coordinate system is a system for assigning an n-tuple of numbers or scalars to each point in an n-dimensional space.
Intersection	In mathematics, the intersection of two sets A and B is the set that contains all elements of A that also belong to B (or equivalently, all elements of B that also belong to A), but no other elements.

Go to **Cram101.com** for the Practice Tests for this Chapter.

Interval	In elementary algebra, an interval is a set that contains every real number between two indicated numbers and may contain the two numbers themselves.
Product	In mathematics, a product is the result of multiplying, or an expression that identifies factors to be multiplied.
Graph of a function	In mathematics, the graph of a function f is the collection of all ordered pairs . In particular, graph means the graphical representation of this collection, in the form of a curve or surface, together with axes, etc. Graphing on a Cartesian plane is sometimes referred to as curve sketching.
Rectangle	In geometry, a rectangle is defined as a quadrilateral where all four of its angles are right angles.
Curve	In mathematics, the concept of a curve tries to capture the intuitive idea of a geometrical one-dimensional and continuous object. A simple example is the circle.
Bounded	In mathematical analysis and related areas of mathematics, a set is called bounded, if it is, in a certain sense, of finite size.
Function	The mathematical concept of a function expresses the intuitive idea of deterministic dependence between two quantities, one of which is viewed as primary and the other as secondary. A function then is a way to associate a unique output for each input of a specified type, for example, a real number or an element of a given set.
Sum	A sum is the result of the addition of a set of numbers. The numbers may be natural numbers, complex numbers, matrices, or still more complicated objects. An infinite sum is a subtle procedure known as a series.
Horizontal	In astronomy, geography, geometry and related sciences and contexts, a plane is said to be horizontal at a given point if it is locally perpendicular to the gradient of the gravity field, i.e., with the direction of the gravitational force at that point.
Integral	The integral of a function is an extension of the concept of a sum, and are identified or found through the use of integration.
Riemann sum	Riemann sum is a method for approximating the values of integrals.
Intersection	In mathematics, the intersection of two sets A and B is the set that contains all elements of A that also belong to B (or equivalently, all elements of B that also belong to A), but no other elements.
Curves	In mathematics, curves are the intuitive idea of a geometrical one-dimensional and continuous object.
Even function	Even function are functions which satisfy particular symmetry relations, with respect to taking additive inverses.
Integrand	Integrand is a function that extends the concept of an ordinary sum
Parabola	In mathematics, the parabola is a conic section generated by the intersection of a right circular conical surface and a plane parallel to a generating straight line of that surface. It can also be defined as locus of points in a plane which are equidistant from a given point.
Range	In mathematics, the range of a function is the set of all "output" values produced by that function. Given a function f :A $\rightarrow$ B, the range of class="unicode">f, is defined to be the set {x class="unicode"> B:x= class="unicode">f(a) for some a

Go to **Cram101.com** for the Practice Tests for this Chapter.

class="unicode">   A}.

Sine	Sine is a trigonemtric function that is important when studying triangles and modeling periodic phenomena, among other applications.
Graphs	Graphs are the basic objects of study in graph theory. Informally speaking, a graph is a set of objects called points, nodes, or vertices connected by links called lines or edges.
Triangle	A triangle is one of the basic shapes of geometry: a polygon with three vertices and three sides which are straight line segments.
Vertex	In geometry, a vertex is a special kind of point, usually a corner of a polygon, polyhedron, or higher dimensional polytope. In the geometry of curves a vertex is a point of where the first derivative of curvature is zero. In graph theory, a vertex is the fundamental unit out of which graphs are formed
Integration	Integration is a process of combining or accumulating. It may also refer to:
Trapezoid	A trapezoid is a quadrilateral, which is defined as a shape with four sides, which has a pair of parallel sides.
Constant	In mathematics and the mathematical sciences, a constant is a fixed, but possibly unspecified, value. This is in contrast to a variable, which is not fixed.
Definite integral	definite integral is an extension of the concept of a sum.
Quadrant	A Quadrant consists of one quarter of the coordinate plane.
Circle	In Euclidean geometry, a circle is the set of all points in a plane at a fixed distance, called the radius, from a given point, the center.
Cross section	In geometry, a cross section is the intersection of a body in 2-dimensional space with a line, or of a body in 3-dimensional space with a plane
Ratio	A ratio is a quantity that denotes the proportional amount or magnitude of one quantity relative to another.
Coordinate	A coordinate is a set of numbers that designate location in a given reference system, such as x,y in a planar coordinate system or an x,y,z in a three-dimensional coordinate system.
Axes	An axes is when two lines intersect somewhere on a plane creating a right angle at intersection
Measure	A measure is a function that assigns a number to subsets of a given set.
Distribution	In mathematical analysis, distribution are objects which generalize functions and probability distributions.
Continuous	A continuous function is a function for which, intuitively, small changes in the input result in small changes in the output.
Equality	Two mathematical objects are equal if and only if they are precisely the same in every way. This defines a binary relation, equality, denoted by the sign of equality "=" in such a way that the statement "x = y" means that x and y are equal.
Coefficient	In mathematics, a coefficient is a constant multiplicative factor of a certain object. The object can be such things as a variable, a vector, a function, etc. For example, the coefficient of $9x^2$ is 9.
Index	The word index is used in a variety of ways in mathematics.
Inequality	In mathematics, an inequality is a statement about the relative size or order of two objects.

Go to **Cram101.com** for the Practice Tests for this Chapter.

Data	Data is a synonym for information.
Characteristic	The characteristic of a ring R is defined to be the smallest positive integer n such that $n\,a = 0$, for all a in R.
Solid	In mathematics, solid geometry was the traditional name for the geometry of three-dimensional Euclidean space — for practical purposes the kind of space we live in.
Cylinder	In mathematics, a cylinder is a quadric surface, with the following equation in Cartesian coordinates: $(x/_a)^2 + (y/_b)^2 = 1$.
Axis	An axis is a straight line around which a geometric figure can be rotated.
Perpendicular	In geometry, two lines or planes if one falls on the other in such a way as to create congruent adjacent angles. The term may be used as a noun or adjective. Thus, referring to Figure 1, the line AB is the perpendicular to CD through the point B.
Plane	In mathematics, a plane is a two-dimensional manifold or surface that is perfectly flat.
Volume	The volume of a solid object is the three-dimensional concept of how much space it occupies, often quantified numerically.
Proof	In mathematics, a proof is a demonstration that, assuming certain axioms, some statement is necessarily true.
Partition	Generally, a partition is a splitting of something into parts.
Average	In mathematics, an average, mean, or central tendency of a data set refers to a measure of the "middle" or "expected" value of the data set.
Mean	The mean, the average in everyday English, which is also called the arithmetic mean (and is distinguished from the geometric mean or harmonic mean). The average is also called the sample mean. The expected value of a random variable, which is also called the population mean.
Theorem	In mathematics, a theorem is a statement that can be proved on the basis of explicitly stated or previously agreed assumptions.
Square	In plane geometry, a square is a polygon with four equal sides, four right angles, and parallel opposite sides. In algebra, the square of a number is that number multiplied by itself.
Ellipse	In mathematics, an ellipse .
Altitude	In geometry, an altitude of a triangle is a straight line through a vertex and perpendicular to (i.e. forming a right angle with) the opposite side or an extension of the opposite side.
Isosceles	An Isosceles triange is a triangle with at least two sides of equal length.
Radius	In classical geometry, a radius of a circle or sphere is any line segment from its center to its boundary. By extension, the radius of a circle or sphere is the length of any such segment. The radius is half the diameter. In science and engineering the term radius of curvature is commonly used as a synonym for radius.
Sphere	In mathematics, a sphere is the set of all points in three-dimensional space (R^3) which are at distance r from a fixed point of that space, where r is a positive real number called the radius of the sphere. The fixed point is called the center or centre, and is not part of the sphere itself.
Cone	A cone is a three-dimensional geometric shape formed by straight lines through a fixed point (vertex) to the points of a fixed curve (directrix)
Equilateral	In geometry, an equilateral polygon is a polygon which has all sides of the same length.

Go to **Cram101.com** for the Practice Tests for this Chapter.

Equilateral triangle	An Equilateral Triangle is a triangle in which all sides are of equal length.
Hypotenuse	The hypotenuse of a right triangle is the triangle's longest side; the side opposite the right angle.
Right triangle	Right triangle has one 90° internal angle a right angle.
Truncated pyramid	Truncated pyramid is the portion of a solid – normally a cone or pyramid – which lies between two parallel planes cutting the solid.
Right circular cone	right circular cone is a three-dimensional geometric shape formed by straight lines through a fixed point vertex to the points of a fixed curve directrix.
Units	The units of measurement are a globally standardized and modernized form of the metric system.
Equator	The equator is an imaginary line on the Earth's surface equidistant from the North Pole and South Pole.
Planes	In mathematics, planes are two-dimensional manifolds or surfaces that are perfectly flat.
Diameter	In geometry, a diameter (Greek words diairo = divide and metro = measure) of a circle is any straight line segment that passes through the centre and whose endpoints are on the circular boundary, or, in more modern usage, the length of such a line segment. When using the word in the more modern sense, one speaks of the diameter rather than a diameter, because all diameters of a circle have the same length. This length is twice the radius. The diameter of a circle is also the longest chord that the circle has.
Minutes	Minutes are a measure of time.
Infinite	infinite is the state of being greater than any finite real or natural number, however large.
Finite	In mathematics, a set is called finite if there is a bijection between the set and some set of the form {1, 2, ..., n} where n is a natural number.
Nonnegative	The nonnegative integers are all the integers from zero on upwards.
Rotation	A rotation is a movement of an object in a circular motion. A two-dimensional object rotates around a center (or point) of rotation. A three-dimensional object rotates around a line called an axis. If the axis of rotation is within the body, the body is said to rotate upon itself, or spin—which implies relative speed and perhaps free-movement with angular momentum. A circular motion about an external point, e.g. the Earth about the Sun, is called an orbit or more properly an orbital revolution.
Continuous function	A continuous function is a function for which, intuitively, small changes in the input result in small changes in the output.
Segment	In geometry, a line segment is a part of a line that is bounded by two end points, and contains every point on the line between its end points.
Shell method	shell method is a means of calculating the volume of a solid of revolution, when integrating along an axis perpendicular to the axis of revolution.
Lateral	A lateral surface is the surface or face of a solid on its sides. It can also be defined as any face or surface that is not a base.
Line segment	A line segment is a part of a line that is bounded by two end points, and contains every point on the line between its end points.
Boundaries	In topology, the boundaries are subsets S of a topological space X is the set of points which can be approached both from S and from the outside of S.

Go to **Cram101.com** for the Practice Tests for this Chapter.

Calculation	A calculation is a deliberate process for transforming one or more inputs into one or more results.
Center	In geometry, the center of an object is a point in some sense in the middle of the object.
Antiderivative	An antiderivative of a function f is a function F whose derivative is equal to f, i.e., F′ = f.
Torus	In geometry, a torus is a surface of revolution generated by revolving a circle in three dimensional space about an axis coplanar with the circle, which does not touch the circle. Examples of tori include the surfaces of doughnuts and inner tubes. A circle rotated about a chord of the circle is called a torus in some contexts, but this is not a common usage in mathematics. The shape produced when a circle is rotated about a chord resembles a round cushion. Torus was the Latin word for a cushion of this shape.
Calculus	Calculus is a mathematical subject that includes the study of limits, derivatives, integrals, and power series and constitutes a major part of modern university curriculum.
Fundamental theorem	In number theory, the fundamental theorem of arithmetic (or unique factorization theorem) states that every natural number greater than 1 can be written as a unique product of prime numbers.
Fundamental Theorem of Calculus	Fundamental Theorem of Calculus of calculus is the statement that the two central operations of calculus, differentiation and integration, are inverse operations: if a continuous function is first integrated and then differentiated, the original function is retrieved.
Center of mass	In physics, the center of mass of a system of particles is a specific point at which, for many purposes, the system's mass behaves as if it were concentrated.
Centroid	In geometry, the centroid or barycenter of an object X in n-dimensional space is the intersection of all hyperplanes that divide X into two parts of equal moment about the hyperplane
Mass	Mass is the property of a physical object that quantifies the amount of matter and energy it is equivalent to.
Principle	A principle signifies a point or points of probability on a subject e.g., the principle of creativity, which allows for the formation of rule or norm or law by interpretation of the phenomena events that can be created.
Symmetry	Symmetry means "constancy", i.e. if something retains a certain feature even after we change a way of looking at it, then it is symmetric.
Axis of symmetry	Axis of symmetry of a two-dimensional figure is a line such that, if a perpendicular is constructed, any two points lying on the perpendicular at equal distances from the axis of symmetry are identical.
Union	In set theory and other branches of mathematics, the union of a collection of sets is the set that contains everything that belongs to any of the sets, but nothing else.
Corollary	A corollary is a mathematical statement which follows easily from a previously proven statement, typically a mathematical theorem.
Pappus of Alexandria	Pappus of Alexandria was a Hellenized Egyptian born in Alexandria, Egypt. He is best known for his work, Synagoge. It is a compendium of mathematics of which eight volumes survive. It covers a wide range of topics, including geometry, recreational mathematics, doubling the cube, polygons and polyhedra.
Circumference	The circumference is the distance around a closed curve. Circumference is a kind of perimeter.

Go to **Cram101.com** for the Practice Tests for this Chapter.

Arc	In Euclidean geometry, an arc is a closed segment of a differentiable curve in the two-dimensional plane; for example, a circular arc is a segment of a circle.
Ring	In mathematics, a ring is an algebraic structure in which addition and multiplication are defined and have properties listed below.
Density	Density is mass m per unit volume V.
Triple	In mathematics, a triple is an n-tuple with n being 3.
Force	In physics, force is an influence that may cause an object to accelerate. It may be experienced as a lift, a push, or a pull. The actual acceleration of the body is determined by the vector sum of all forces acting on it, known as net force or resultant force.
Opposite	In mathematics, the additive inverse, or opposite of a number n is the number that, when added to n, yields zero. The additive inverse of n is denoted −n. For example, 7 is −7, because 7 + (−7) = 0, and the additive inverse of −0.3 is 0.3, because −0.3 + 0.3 = 0.
Additive inverse	In mathematics, the additive inverse of a number n is the number that, when added to n, yields zero. The additive inverse of n is denoted −n. For example, 7 is −7, because 7 + (−7) = 0, and the additive inverse of −0.3 is 0.3, because −0.3 + 0.3 = 0.
Equilibrium	In economics, economic equilibrium is simply a state of the world where economic forces are balanced and in the absence of external influences the values of economic variables will not change.
Origin	In mathematics, the origin of a coordinate system is the point where the axes of the system intersect.
Newton	Sir Isaac Newton, was an English physicist, mathematician, astronomer, natural philosopher, and alchemist, regarded by many as the greatest figure in the history of science
Joule	Joule is the SI unit of energy.
Kilogram	The kilogram or kilogramme is the SI base unit of mass. It is defined as being equal to the mass of the international prototype of the kilogram.
Acceleration	Acceleration is defined as the rate of change or derivative with respect to time of velocity.
Meter	The metre (or meter, see spelling differences) is a measure of length. It is the basic unit of length in the metric system and in the International System of Units (SI), used around the world for general and scientific purposes.
Metric	In mathematics a metric is a function which defines a distance between elements of a set.
Metric system	The metric system is a decimalized system of measurement based on the metre and the gram.
Sigma	Sigma is the eighteenth letter of the Greek alphabet.
Rate	A rate is a special kind of ratio, indicating a relationship between two measurements with different units, such as miles to gallons or cents to pounds.
Argument	In mathematics, science including computer science, linguistics and engineering, an argument is, generally speaking, an independent variable or input to a function.
Slide	The slide rule, also known as a slipstick, is a mechanical analog computer, consisting of at least two finely divided scales , most often a fixed outer pair and a movable inner one, with a sliding window called the cursor.
Inclined plane	The inclined plane is one of the classical simple machines; as the name suggests, it is a flat surface whose endpoints are at different heights. By moving an object up an inclined plane rather than directly from one height to another, the amount of force required is reduced, at the expense of increasing the distance the object must travel. The mechanical

Go to **Cram101.com** for the Practice Tests for this Chapter.

advantage of an inclined plane is the ratio of the length of the sloped surface to the height it spans; this may also be expressed as the cosecant of the angle between the plane and the horizontal.

Gallon	U.S. liquid gallon is legally defined as 231 cubic inches, and is equal to 3.785411784 litres or abotu 0.13368 cubic feet. This is the most common definition of a gallon. The U.S. fluid ounce is defined as 1/128 of a U.S. gallon.
Variable	A variable is a symbolic representation denoting a quantity or expression. It often represents an "unknown" quantity that has the potential to change.
Velocity	Velocity of an object is its speed in a particular direction.
Mile	A mile is a unit of length, usually used to measure distance, in a number of different systems, including Imperial units, United States customary units and Norwegian/Swedish mil. Its size can vary from system to system, but in each is between 1 and 10 kilometers. In contemporary English contexts mile refers to either:
Measurement	Measurement is the estimation of a physical quantity such as distance, energy, temperature, or time.
Power	Power has many meanings, most of which simply .
Column	In mathematics, a matrix can be thought of as each row or column being a vector. Hence, a space formed by row vectors or column vectors are said to be a row space or a column space.
Midpoint	midpoint is the middle point of a line segment.
Isosceles trapezoid	An isosceles trapezoid (isosceles trapezium in British English) is a quadrilateral with a line of symmetry bisecting one pair of opposite sides, making it automatically a trapezoid. Also, an isosceles trapezoid's base angles are congruent.
Legs	In a right triangle, the legs of the triangle are the two sides that are perpendicular to each other, as opposed to the hypotenuse.
Slope	Slope is often used to describe the measurement of the steepness, incline, gradient, or grade of a straight line. The slope is defined as the ratio of the "rise" divided by the "run" between two points on a line, or in other words, the ratio of the altitude change to the horizontal distance between any two points on the line.
Differential calculus	Differential calculus, a field in mathematics, is the study of how functions change when their inputs change. The primary object of study in differential calculus is the derivative.
Concavity	The word concavity means curving in or hollowed inward.
Springs	Springs are flexible, elastic objects used to store mechanical energy.

Go to **Cram101.com** for the Practice Tests for this Chapter.

Coefficient	In mathematics, a coefficient is a constant multiplicative factor of a certain object. The object can be such things as a variable, a vector, a function, etc. For example, the coefficient of $9x^2$ is 9.
Polynomial	In mathematics, a polynomial is an expression that is constructed from one or more variables and constants, using only the operations of addition, subtraction, multiplication, and constant positive whole number exponents. is a polynomial. Note in particular that division by an expression containing a variable is not in general allowed in polynomials. [1]
Function	The mathematical concept of a function expresses the intuitive idea of deterministic dependence between two quantities, one of which is viewed as primary and the other as secondary. A function then is a way to associate a unique output for each input of a specified type, for example, a real number or an element of a given set.
Transcendental	In mathematics, a transcendental number is a real or complex number which is not algebraic, that is, not a solution of a non-zero polynomial equation, with rational coefficients.
Inverse	Inverse element of an element x with respect to a binary operation * with identity element e is an element y such that $x * y = y * x = e$. In particular,
Domain	In mathematics, a domain of a k-place relation L X_1 × ... × X_k is one of the sets X_i, $1 \le j \le k$. In the special case where k = 2 and L X_1 class="unicode">× X_2 is a function L : X_1 class="unicode">→ X_2, it is conventional to refer to X_1 as the domain of the function and to refer to X_2 as the codomain of the function.
Constant	In mathematics and the mathematical sciences, a constant is a fixed, but possibly unspecified, value. This is in contrast to a variable, which is not fixed.
Constant function	Constant function is a function whose values do not vary and thus are constant.
Quadratic function	A quadratic function is a polynomial function of the form $f(x) = ax^2 + bx + c$, where a, b, c are real numbers and a class="unicode"> , 0.
Cube	A cube is a three-dimensional solid object bounded by six square faces, facets, or sides, with three meeting at each vertex.
Nonnegative	The nonnegative integers are all the integers from zero on upwards.
Square	In plane geometry, a square is a polygon with four equal sides, four right angles, and parallel opposite sides. In algebra, the square of a number is that number multiplied by itself.
Square root	In mathematics, a square root of a number x is a number r such that $r^2 = x$, or in words, a number r whose square (the result of multiplying the number by itself) is x.
Root	In mathematics, a root of a complex-valued function f is a member x of the domain of f such that f(x) vanishes at x, that is, x : f (x) = 0.
Horizontal	In astronomy, geography, geometry and related sciences and contexts, a plane is said to be horizontal at a given point if it is locally perpendicular to the gradient of the gravity field, i.e., with the direction of the gravitational force at that point.
Horizontal line test	horizontal line test is a test used to determine if a function is injective, surjective or bijective.
Test	Acid test ratio measures the ability of a company to use its near cash or quick assets to

Go to **Cram101.com** for the Practice Tests for this Chapter.

immediately extinguish its current liabilities.

Theorem	In mathematics, a theorem is a statement that can be proved on the basis of explicitly stated or previously agreed assumptions.
Proof	In mathematics, a proof is a demonstration that, assuming certain axioms, some statement is necessarily true.
Range	In mathematics, the range of a function is the set of all "output" values produced by that function. Given a function f :A → B, the range of class="unicode">f, is defined to be the set {x class="unicode"> B:x= class="unicode">f(a) for some a class="unicode"> A}.
Notation	Mathematical notation is used to represent ideas.
Inverse function	An inverse function is a function which does the reverse of a given function.
Reciprocal	In mathematics, the multiplicative inverse of a number x, denoted 1/x or x^{-1}, is the number which, when multiplied by x, yields 1. The multiplicative inverse of x is also called the reciprocal of x.
Mean	The mean, the average in everyday English, which is also called the arithmetic mean (and is distinguished from the geometric mean or harmonic mean). The average is also called the sample mean. The expected value of a random variable, which is also called the population mean.
Graphs	Graphs are the basic objects of study in graph theory. Informally speaking, a graph is a set of objects called points, nodes, or vertices connected by links called lines or edges.
Calculation	A calculation is a deliberate process for transforming one or more inputs into one or more results.
Symbols	Symbols are objects, characters, or other concrete representations of ideas, concepts, or other abstractions.
Linear	The word linear comes from the Latin word linearis, which means created by lines.
Linear function	A linear function is a first degree polynomial mathematical function of the form: f(x) = mx + b where m and b are real constants and x is a real variable.
Derivative	The derivative is a measurement of how a function changes when the values of its inputs change.
Scale	In Euclidean geometry, a uniform scale is a linear transformation that enlargers or diminishes objects, and whose scale factor is the same in all directions. This is also called homothethy.
Chain rule	In calculus, the chain rule is a formula for the derivative of the composite of two functions.
Reflection	In mathematics, a reflection (also spelled reflexion) is a map that transforms an object into its mirror image.
Differential calculus	Differential calculus, a field in mathematics, is the study of how functions change when their inputs change. The primary object of study in differential calculus is the derivative.
Tangent	In trigonometry, the tangent is a function defined as tan x = $\sin x$/$_{\cos}$ x. The function is so-named because it can be defined as the length of a certain segment of a tangent (in the geometric sense) to the unit circle. In plane geometry, a line

Go to **Cram101.com** for the Practice Tests for this Chapter.

is tangent to a curve, at some point, if both line and curve pass through the point with the same direction.

Tangent line

Tangent line has two distinct but etymologically-related meanings: one in geometry and one in trigonometry.

Slope

Slope is often used to describe the measurement of the steepness, incline, gradient, or grade of a straight line. The slope is defined as the ratio of the "rise" divided by the "run" between two points on a line, or in other words, the ratio of the altitude change to the horizontal distance between any two points on the line.

Intersecting

In geometry, intersecting lines are two lines that share one or more common points.

Leibniz

Leibniz was a German mathematician and philosopher. He invented calculus independently of Newton, and his notation is the one in general use since.

Leibniz notation

Leibniz notation named in honor of the 17th century German philosopher and mathematician Gottfried Wilhelm Leibniz, was originally the use of expressions such as dx and dy and to represent "infinitely small" or infinitesimal increments of quantities x and y, just as $\ddot{A}$x and $\ddot{A}$y represent finite increments of x and y respectively.

Rate

A rate is a special kind of ratio, indicating a relationship between two measurements with different units, such as miles to gallons or cents to pounds.

Composition

In mathematics, a composition of a positive integer n is a way of writing n as a sum of positive integers.

Composition of two

The composition of two functions is determined by the nesting of two or more functions to form a single new function.

Continuous

A continuous function is a function for which, intuitively, small changes in the input result in small changes in the output.

Number system

number system is a set of numbers, in the broadest sense of the word, together with one or more operations, such as addition or multiplication.

Logarithm

In mathematics, a logarithm of a number x is the exponent y of the power by such that x = b^y. The value used for the base b must be neither 0 nor 1, nor a root of 1 in the case of the extension to complex numbers, and is typically 10, e, or 2.

Power

Power has many meanings, most of which simply .

Calculus

Calculus is a mathematical subject that includes the study of limits, derivatives, integrals, and power series and constitutes a major part of modern university curriculum.

Multiplication

In mathematics, multiplication is an elementary arithmetic operation. When one of the numbers is a whole number, multiplication is the repeated sum of the other number.

Product

In mathematics, a product is the result of multiplying, or an expression that identifies factors to be multiplied.

Sum

A sum is the result of the addition of a set of numbers. The numbers may be natural numbers, complex numbers, matrices, or still more complicated objects. An infinite sum is a subtle procedure known as a series.

Central

Central is an adjective usually refering to being in the centre.

Quotient

In mathematics, a quotient is the end result of a division problem. It can also be expressed as the number of times the divisor divides into the dividend.

Difference quotient

The function difference divided by the point difference is known as the Difference quotient

Denominator	A denominator is the part of a fraction that tells how many equal parts make up a whole, and which is used in the name of the fraction: "halves", "thirds", "fourths" or "quarters", "fifths" and so on.
Rational	In mathematics, a rational number is a number which can be expressed as a ratio of two integers. Non-integer rational numbers (commonly called fractions) are usually written as the vulgar fraction a / b, where b is not zero.
Statement	In common philosophical language, a proposition or statement, is the content of an assertion, that is, it is true-or-false and defined by the meaning of a particular piece of language.
Interval	In elementary algebra, an interval is a set that contains every real number between two indicated numbers and may contain the two numbers themselves.
Multiple	A multiple of a number is the product of that number with any integer.
Greater than	In mathematics, an inequality is a statement about the relative size or order of two objects. For example 14 > 10, or 14 is greater than 10.
Expansion	An expansion of a product of sums expresses it as a sum of products by using the fact that multiplication distributes over addition.
Irrationality	In mathematics, Irrationality (i.e. an irrational number) occurs when any real number that is not a rational number — that is, it is a number which cannot be expressed as m/n, where m and n are integers.
Curve	In mathematics, the concept of a curve tries to capture the intuitive idea of a geometrical one-dimensional and continuous object. A simple example is the circle.
Differential	A differential is traditionally an infinitesimally small change in a variable.
Euler	Leonhard Euler was a pioneering Swiss mathematician and physicist, who spent most of his life in Russia and Germany.
Intermediate Value Theorem	The Intermediate Value theorem implies that on any great circle around the world, the temperature, pressure, elevation, carbon dioxide concentration, or anything else that varies continuously, there will always exist two antipodal points that share the same value for that variable.
Even function	Even function are functions which satisfy particular symmetry relations, with respect to taking additive inverses.
Image	In mathematics, image is a part of the set theoretic notion of function.
Intercept	Any point where a graph makes contact with an coordinate axis is called an intercept of the graph
Concavity	The word concavity means curving in or hollowed inward.
Asymptote	An asymptote is a straight line or curve A to which another curve B approaches closer and closer as one moves along it. As one moves along B, the space between it and the asymptote A becomes smaller and smaller, and can in fact be made as small as one could wish by going far enough along. A curve may or may not touch or cross its asymptote. In fact, the curve may intersect the asymptote an infinite number of times.
Vertical asymptote	Vertical asymptote is a straight line or curve A to which another curve B the one being studied approaches closer and closer as one moves along it.
Integral	The integral of a function is an extension of the concept of a sum, and are identified or found through the use of integration.
Integration	Integration is a process of combining or accumulating. It may also refer to:

Check	A check is a negotiable instrument instructing a financial institution to pay a specific amount of a specific currency from a specific demand account held in the maker/depositor face=symbol>¢s name with that institution. Both the maker and payee may be natural persons or legal entities.
Antiderivative	An antiderivative of a function f is a function F whose derivative is equal to f, i.e., F′ = f.
Numerator	A numerator is a numeral used to indicate a count. The most common use of the word today is to name the part of a fraction that tells the number or count of equal parts.
Integrand	Integrand is a function that extends the concept of an ordinary sum
Solution set	A solution set is a set of possible values that a variable can take on in order to satisfy a given set of conditions, which may include equations and inequalities.
Valid	In statistics, a valid measure is one which is measuring what is supposed to measure.
Product rule	The product rule governs the differentiation of products of differentiable functions.
Explicit formula	In mathematics, the explicit formula(e) for L-functions are a class of summation formulae, expressing sums taken over the complex number zeroes of a given L-function, typically in terms of quantities studied by number theory by use of the theory of special functions.
Factors	In mathematics, factorization (British English: factorisation) or factoring is the decomposition of an object (for example, a number, a polynomial, or a matrix) into a product of other objects, or factors, which when multiplied together give the original.
Curves	In mathematics, curves are the intuitive idea of a geometrical one-dimensional and continuous object.
Bounded	In mathematical analysis and related areas of mathematics, a set is called bounded, if it is, in a certain sense, of finite size.
Quadrant	A Quadrant consists of one quarter of the coordinate plane.
Acceleration	Acceleration is defined as the rate of change or derivative with respect to time of velocity.
Quotient rule	The quotient rule is a method of finding the derivative of a function that is the quotient of two other functions for which derivatives exist.
Extreme value	The term extreme value refers to the largest and the smallest element of a set.
Average	In mathematics, an average, mean, or central tendency of a data set refers to a measure of the "middle" or "expected" value of the data set.
Exponential	In mathematics, exponential growth occurs when the growth rate of a function is always proportional to the function's current size.
Exponential function	Exponential function is one of the most important functions in mathematics. A function commonly used to study growth and decay
Extremum	In mathematics, maxima and minima, known collectively as extrema, are the largest value maximum or smallest value minimum, that a function takes in a point either within a given neighborhood local extremum or on the function domain in its entirety global extremum.
Velocity	Velocity of an object is its speed in a particular direction.
Intersection	In mathematics, the intersection of two sets A and B is the set that contains all elements of A that also belong to B (or equivalently, all elements of B that also belong to A), but no other elements.
Expression	An expression is a combination of numbers, operators, grouping symbols and/or free variables

Go to **Cram101.com** for the Practice Tests for this Chapter.

and bound variables arranged in a meaningful way which can be evaluated..

Irrational

In mathematics, an irrational number is any real number that is not a rational number- that is, it is a number which cannot be expressed as a fraction m/n, where m and n are integers.

Identity

An identity is an equality that remains true regardless of the values of any variables that appear within it, to distinguish it from an equality which is true under more particular conditions.

Equating

equating traditionally refers to the statistical process of determining comparable scores on different forms of an exam

Corollary

A corollary is a mathematical statement which follows easily from a previously proven statement, typically a mathematical theorem.

Engineering

Engineering is the design, analysis, and/or construction of works for practical purposes.

Physics

Physics, Greek for "knowledge of nature," is the branch of science concerned with the discovery and characterization of universal laws which govern matter, energy, space, and time.

Symmetry

Symmetry means "constancy", i.e. if something retains a certain feature even after we change a way of looking at it, then it is symmetric.

Probability

Probability is the chance that something is likely to happen or be the case.

Statistics

Statistics is a mathematical science pertaining to the collection, analysis, interpretation or explanation, and presentation of data. It is applicable to a wide variety of academic disciplines, from the physical and social sciences to the humanities.

Coordinate

A coordinate is a set of numbers that designate location in a given reference system, such as x,y in a planar coordinate system or an x,y,z in a three-dimensional coordinate system.

Origin

In mathematics, the origin of a coordinate system is the point where the axes of the system intersect.

Proportional

In mathematics, two quantities are called proportional if they vary in such a way that one of the quantities is a constant multiple of the other, or equivalently if they have a constant ratio.

Vertex

In geometry, a vertex is a special kind of point, usually a corner of a polygon, polyhedron, or higher dimensional polytope. In the geometry of curves a vertex is a point of where the first derivative of curvature is zero. In graph theory, a vertex is the fundamental unit out of which graphs are formed

Rectangle

In geometry, a rectangle is defined as a quadrilateral where all four of its angles are right angles.

Volume

The volume of a solid object is the three-dimensional concept of how much space it occupies, often quantified numerically.

Solid

In mathematics, solid geometry was the traditional name for the geometry of three-dimensional Euclidean space — for practical purposes the kind of space we live in.

Shell method

shell method is a means of calculating the volume of a solid of revolution, when integrating along an axis perpendicular to the axis of revolution.

Definite integral

definite integral is an extension of the concept of a sum.

Conjecture

In mathematics, a conjecture is a mathematical statement which appears likely to be true, but has not been formally proven to be true under the rules of mathematical logic.

Rational Number	In mathematics, a rational number is a number which can be expressed as a ratio of two integers. Non-integer rational numbers (commonly called fractions) are usually written as the vulgar fraction a / b, where b is not zero.
Exponentiating	Exponentiating is a mathematical operation, written a^n, involving two numbers, the base a and the exponent n.
Exponentiation	Exponentiation is a mathematical operation, written a^n, involving two numbers, the base a and the exponent n.
Variable	A variable is a symbolic representation denoting a quantity or expression. It often represents an "unknown" quantity that has the potential to change.
Interest	Interest is the fee paid on borrowed money.
Natural logarithm	Natural logarithm is the logarithm to the base e, where e is an irrational constant approximately equal to 2.718281828459.
Exponential growth	In mathematics, exponential growth occurs when the growth rate of a function is always proportional to the function's current size.
Period	In business, particularly accounting, a period is the time intervals that the accounts, statement, payments, or other calculations cover.
Amount	amount is a kind of property which exists as magnitude or multitude. It is among the basic classes of things along with quality, substance, change, and relation.
Additive	In mathematics, the additive inverse, or opposite, of a number n is the number that, when added to n, yields zero. The additive inverse of n is denoted −n.
Multiplicative	In mathematics, the multiplicative inverse of a number x, denoted 1/x or x^{-1}, is the number which, when multiplied by x, yields 1. The multiplicative inverse of x is also called the reciprocal of x.
Coterminal	Initial objects are also called coterminal, and terminal objects are also called final.
Space	Space is a set, with some particular properties and usually some additional structure, such as the operations of addition or multiplication, for instance.
Population	In sociology and biology a population is the collection of people or organisms of a particular species living in a given geographic area or space, usually measured by a census.
Population growth	Population growth is change in population over time, and can be quantified as the change in the number of individuals in a population per unit time.
Equivalent	Equivalence is the condition of being equivalent or essentially equal.
World population	The world population is the total number of human beings alive on the planet Earth at a given time.
Radioactive decay	Radioactive decay is the process in which an unstable atomic nucleus loses energy by emitting radiation in the form of particles or electromagnetic waves.
Sample	sample is a subset of a population.
Limiting	limiting Any process by which a specified characteristic usually amplitude of the output of a device is prevented from exceeding a predetermined value.
Interest rate	An interest rate is the fee paid on borrow money.
Investment	Investment or investing is a term with several closely-related meanings in business management, finance and economics, related to saving or deferring consumption.
Nominal	nominal generally derives from name. A nominal quantity e.g., length, diameter, volume,

voltage, value is generally the quantity according to which some item has been named or is generally referred to.

Increment
An increment is an increase, either of some fixed amount, for example added regularly, or of a variable amount.

Compound
Compound interest refers to the fact that whenever interest is calculated, it is based not only on the original principal, but also on any unpaid interest that has been added to the principal.

Compound interest
Compound interest refers to the fact that whenever interest is calculated, it is based not only on the original principal, but also on any unpaid interest that has been added to the principal. The more frequently interest is compounded, the faster the balance grows.

Squeeze Theorem
In calculus, the squeeze theorem is a theorem regarding the limit of a function. The theorem asserts that if two functions approach the same limit at a point, and if a third function is "squeezed" between those functions, then the third function also approaches that limit at that point.

Doubling time
The doubling time is the period of time required for a quantity to double in size or value.

Estimating
The act of Estimating is the calculated approximation of a result which is usable even if input data may be incomplete, uncertain, or noisy.

Divisor
In mathematics, a divisor of an integer n, also called a factor of n, is an integer which evenly divides n without leaving a remainder.

Triple
In mathematics, a triple is an n-tuple with n being 3.

Experiment
In the scientific method, an experiment (Latin: ex-+-periri, "of (or from) trying"), is a set of actions and observations, performed in the context of solving a particular problem or question, in order to support or falsify a hypothesis or research concerning phenomena.

Data
Data is a synonym for information.

Prediction
A prediction is a statement or claimt that a particular event will occur in the future in more certain terms than a forecast.

Mile
A mile is a unit of length, usually used to measure distance, in a number of different systems, including Imperial units, United States customary units and Norwegian/Swedish mil. Its size can vary from system to system, but in each is between 1 and 10 kilometers. In contemporary English contexts mile refers to either:

Minutes
Minutes are a measure of time.

Meter
The metre (or meter, see spelling differences) is a measure of length. It is the basic unit of length in the metric system and in the International System of Units (SI), used around the world for general and scientific purposes.

Altitude
In geometry, an altitude of a triangle is a straight line through a vertex and perpendicular to (i.e. forming a right angle with) the opposite side or an extension of the opposite side.

Present value
present value of a single or multiple future payments is the nominal amounts of money to change hands at some future date, discounted to account for the time value of money, and other factors such as investment risk.

Future value
future value measures the nominal future sum of money that a given sum of money is "worth" at a specified time in the future assuming a certain interest rate; this value does not include corrections for inflation or other factors that affect the true value of money in the future.

Miles per hour
Miles per hour is a unit of speed, expressing the number of international miles covered per hour.

Go to **Cram101.com** for the Practice Tests for this Chapter.
And, **NEVER** highlight a book again!

Radiocarbon dating	Radiocarbon dating is a radiometric dating method that uses the naturally occurring isotope carbon-14 to determine the age of carbonaceous materials up to about 60,000 years.
Ratio	A ratio is a quantity that denotes the proportional amount or magnitude of one quantity relative to another.
Trigonometric	In mathematics, the trigonometric functions are functions of an angle; they are important when studying triangles and modeling periodic phenomena, among many other applications.
Trigonometric functions	The trigonometric functions are functions of an angle; they are important when studying triangles and modeling periodic phenomena, among many other applications.
Inverse trigonometric functions	In mathematics, the inverse trigonometric functions are the inverse functions of the trigonometric functions.
Sine	Sine is a trigonemtric function that is important when studying triangles and modeling periodic phenomena, among other applications.
Arc	In Euclidean geometry, an arc is a closed segment of a differentiable curve in the two-dimensional plane; for example, a circular arc is a segment of a circle.
Radian	The radian is a unit of plane angle. It is represented by the symbol "rad" or, more rarely, by the superscript c (for "circular measure"). For example, an angle of 1.2 radians would be written "1.2 rad" or "1.2c" (second symbol can produce confusion with centigrads).
Radian measure	radian measure is a unit of plane angle, equal to 180/ð degrees, or about 57.2958 degrees
Measure	A measure is a function that assigns a number to subsets of a given set.
Acute	Angles smaller than a right angle are called acute angles (less than 90 degrees).
Real number	In mathematics, a real number may be described informally as a number that can be given by an infinite decimal representation.
Secant	Secant is a trigonometric function that is the reciprocal of cosine.
Cosecant	Cosecant is a term in Trigonometry used to describe the secant of the complement of a cirlce.
Cosine	The cosine of an angle is the ratio of the length of the adjacent side to the length of the hypotenuse.
Cotangent	Cotangent is the ratio of the adjacent to the opposite side of a right-angeled triangle
Cofunction	In mathematics, a function f is cofunction of a function g if f whenever A and B are complementary angles. This definition typically applies to trigonometric functions.
Triangle	A triangle is one of the basic shapes of geometry: a polygon with three vertices and three sides which are straight line segments.
Right triangle	Right triangle has one 90° internal angle a right angle.
Perpendicular	In geometry, two lines or planes if one falls on the other in such a way as to create congruent adjacent angles. The term may be used as a noun or adjective. Thus, referring to Figure 1, the line AB is the perpendicular to CD through the point B.
Partition	Generally, a partition is a splitting of something into parts.
Travel	Travel is the transport of people on a trip/journey or the process or time involved in a person or object moving from one location to another.
Light	Light is electromagnetic radiation with a wavelength that is visible to the eye (visible light) or, in a technical or scientific context, electromagnetic radiation of any wavelength.

Speed of light	The speed of light in a vacuum is an important physical constant denoted by the letter c for constant or the Latin word celeritas meaning "swiftness
Index	The word index is used in a variety of ways in mathematics.
Incidence	In geometry, the relations of incidence are those such as 'lies on' between points and lines (as in 'point P lies on line L'), and 'intersects face=symbol>¢ (as in 'line L_1 intersects line L_2', in three-dimensional space). That is, they are the binary relations describing how subsets meet.
Plane	In mathematics, a plane is a two-dimensional manifold or surface that is perfectly flat.
Ray	A ray given two distinct points A and B on the ray, is the set of points C on the line containing points A and B such that A is not strictly between C and B.
Combination	In combinatorial mathematics, a combination is an un-ordered collection of unique elements.
Turn	A turn is 360° or 2ð radians.
Hyperbolic function	A hyperbolic function is an analog of an ordinary trigonometric, or circular, function.
Tension	Tension is a reaction force applied by a stretched string on the objects which stretch it.
Density	Density is mass m per unit volume V.
Force	In physics, force is an influence that may cause an object to accelerate. It may be experienced as a lift, a push, or a pull. The actual acceleration of the body is determined by the vector sum of all forces acting on it, known as net force or resultant force.
Catenary	Catenary is the shape of a hanging flexible chain or cable when supported at its ends and acted upon by a uniform gravitational force. The chain is steepest near the points of suspension because this part of the chain has the most weight pulling down on it. Toward the bottom, the slope of the chain decreases because the chain is supporting less weight.
Center	In geometry, the center of an object is a point in some sense in the middle of the object.
Coordinate system	In mathematics and its applications, a coordinate system is a system for assigning an n-tuple of numbers or scalars to each point in an n-dimensional space.
Proportionality	Proportionality is a special mathematical relationship between two quantities.Two quantities are called proportional if they vary in such a way that one of the quantities is a constant multiple of the other, or equivalently if they have a constant ratio.
Rule of 72	In finance, the rule of 72, the rule of 71, the rule of 70 and the rule of 69.3 all refer to a method for estimating an investment's doubling time, or halving time. These rules apply to exponential growth and decay respectively, and are therefore used for compound interest as opposed to simple interest calculations.

Go to **Cram101.com** for the Practice Tests for this Chapter.

Constant	In mathematics and the mathematical sciences, a constant is a fixed, but possibly unspecified, value. This is in contrast to a variable, which is not fixed.
Integral	The integral of a function is an extension of the concept of a sum, and are identified or found through the use of integration.
Sine	Sine is a trigonemtric function that is important when studying triangles and modeling periodic phenomena, among other applications.
Coordinate	A coordinate is a set of numbers that designate location in a given reference system, such as x,y in a planar coordinate system or an x,y,z in a three-dimensional coordinate system.
Coordinate system	In mathematics and its applications, a coordinate system is a system for assigning an n-tuple of numbers or scalars to each point in an n-dimensional space.
Graphs	Graphs are the basic objects of study in graph theory. Informally speaking, a graph is a set of objects called points, nodes, or vertices connected by links called lines or edges.
Bounded	In mathematical analysis and related areas of mathematics, a set is called bounded, if it is, in a certain sense, of finite size.
Intersection	In mathematics, the intersection of two sets A and B is the set that contains all elements of A that also belong to B (or equivalently, all elements of B that also belong to A), but no other elements.
Interval	In elementary algebra, an interval is a set that contains every real number between two indicated numbers and may contain the two numbers themselves.
Units	The units of measurement are a globally standardized and modernized form of the metric system.
Volume	The volume of a solid object is the three-dimensional concept of how much space it occupies, often quantified numerically.
Solid	In mathematics, solid geometry was the traditional name for the geometry of three-dimensional Euclidean space — for practical purposes the kind of space we live in.
Cubic units	Cubic units are cubes in which all sides are of the same length and all face perpendicular to each other including an atom at each corner of the unigt cell.
Product	In mathematics, a product is the result of multiplying, or an expression that identifies factors to be multiplied.
Integration	Integration is a process of combining or accumulating. It may also refer to:
Derivative	The derivative is a measurement of how a function changes when the values of its inputs change.
Curve	In mathematics, the concept of a curve tries to capture the intuitive idea of a geometrical one-dimensional and continuous object. A simple example is the circle.
Proper	A proper fraction is a fraction in which the absolute value of the numerator is less than the denominator--hence, the absolute value of the fraction is less than 1.
Antiderivative	An antiderivative of a function f is a function F whose derivative is equal to f, i.e., $F' = f$.
Trigonometric	In mathematics, the trigonometric functions are functions of an angle; they are important when studying triangles and modeling periodic phenomena, among many other applications.
Trigonometric functions	The trigonometric functions are functions of an angle; they are important when studying triangles and modeling periodic phenomena, among many other applications.

Go to **Cram101.com** for the Practice Tests for this Chapter.

Exponential	In mathematics, exponential growth occurs when the growth rate of a function is always proportional to the function's current size.
Integrand	Integrand is a function that extends the concept of an ordinary sum
Polynomial	In mathematics, a polynomial is an expression that is constructed from one or more variables and constants, using only the operations of addition, subtraction, multiplication, and constant positive whole number exponents. is a polynomial. Note in particular that division by an expression containing a variable is not in general allowed in polynomials. [1]
Function	The mathematical concept of a function expresses the intuitive idea of deterministic dependence between two quantities, one of which is viewed as primary and the other as secondary. A function then is a way to associate a unique output for each input of a specified type, for example, a real number or an element of a given set.
Mixture	In chemistry, a mixture is substance made by combining two or more different materials in such a way that no chemical reaction occurs.
Chain rule	In calculus, the chain rule is a formula for the derivative of the composite of two functions.
Theorem	In mathematics, a theorem is a statement that can be proved on the basis of explicitly stated or previously agreed assumptions.
Calculus	Calculus is a mathematical subject that includes the study of limits, derivatives, integrals, and power series and constitutes a major part of modern university curriculum.
Fundamental theorem	In number theory, the fundamental theorem of arithmetic (or unique factorization theorem) states that every natural number greater than 1 can be written as a unique product of prime numbers.
Fundamental Theorem of Calculus	Fundamental Theorem of Calculus of calculus is the statement that the two central operations of calculus, differentiation and integration, are inverse operations: if a continuous function is first integrated and then differentiated, the original function is retrieved.
Logarithm	In mathematics, a logarithm of a number x is the exponent y of the power by such that x = b^y. The value used for the base b must be neither 0 nor 1, nor a root of 1 in the case of the extension to complex numbers, and is typically 10, e, or 2.
Inverse	Inverse element of an element x with respect to a binary operation * with identity element e is an element y such that x * y = y * x = e. In particular,
Inverse trigonometric functions	In mathematics, the inverse trigonometric functions are the inverse functions of the trigonometric functions.
Trigonometric substitution	In mathematics, trigonometric substitution is the substitution of trigonometric functions for other expressions.
Centroid	In geometry, the centroid or barycenter of an object X in n-dimensional space is the intersection of all hyperplanes that divide X into two parts of equal moment about the hyperplane
Axes	An axes is when two lines intersect somewhere on a plane creating a right angle at intersection
Mass	Mass is the property of a physical object that quantifies the amount of matter and energy it is equivalent to.
Density	Density is mass m per unit volume V.
Center	In geometry, the center of an object is a point in some sense in the middle of the object.

Center of mass	In physics, the center of mass of a system of particles is a specific point at which, for many purposes, the system's mass behaves as if it were concentrated.
Reduction	In mathematics, reduction refers to the rewriting of an expression into a simpler form.
Coefficient	In mathematics, a coefficient is a constant multiplicative factor of a certain object. The object can be such things as a variable, a vector, a function, etc. For example, the coefficient of $9x^2$ is 9.
Degree	In mathematics, there are several meanings of degree depending on the subject.
Continuous	A continuous function is a function for which, intuitively, small changes in the input result in small changes in the output.
Identity	An identity is an equality that remains true regardless of the values of any variables that appear within it, to distinguish it from an equality which is true under more particular conditions.
Rate	A rate is a special kind of ratio, indicating a relationship between two measurements with different units, such as miles to gallons or cents to pounds.
Interest	Interest is the fee paid on borrowed money.
Present value	present value of a single or multiple future payments is the nominal amounts of money to change hands at some future date, discounted to account for the time value of money, and other factors such as investment risk.
Interest rate	An interest rate is the fee paid on borrow money.
Investment	Investment or investing is a term with several closely-related meanings in business management, finance and economics, related to saving or deferring consumption.
Future value	future value measures the nominal future sum of money that a given sum of money is "worth" at a specified time in the future assuming a certain interest rate; this value does not include corrections for inflation or other factors that affect the true value of money in the future.
Revenue	Revenue is a business term for the amount of money that a company receives from its activities in a given period, mostly from sales of products and/or services to customers
Partition	Generally, a partition is a splitting of something into parts.
Postulate	The term postulate, or axiom, indicates a starting assumption from which other statements are logically derived.
Cosine	The cosine of an angle is the ratio of the length of the adjacent side to the length of the hypotenuse.
Integers	The integers are the only integral domain whose positive elements are well-ordered, and in which order is preserved by addition. Like the natural numbers, the integers form a countably infinite set. The set of all integers is usually denoted in mathematics by a boldface Z .
Power	Power has many meanings, most of which simply .
Sum	A sum is the result of the addition of a set of numbers. The numbers may be natural numbers, complex numbers, matrices, or still more complicated objects. An infinite sum is a subtle procedure known as a series.
Equivalent	Equivalence is the condition of being equivalent or essentially equal.
Cotangent	Cotangent is the ratio of the adjacent to the opposite side of a right-angled triangle
Tangent	In trigonometry, the tangent is a function defined as $\tan x = {}^{\sin x}/_{\cos}$ x. The function is so-named because it can be defined as the length of a certain

Go to **Cram101.com** for the Practice Tests for this Chapter.

segment of a tangent (in the geometric sense) to the unit circle. In plane geometry, a line is tangent to a curve, at some point, if both line and curve pass through the point with the same direction.

Secant
Secant is a trigonometric function that is the reciprocal of cosine.

Curves
In mathematics, curves are the intuitive idea of a geometrical one-dimensional and continuous object.

Solution set
A solution set is a set of possible values that a variable can take on in order to satisfy a given set of conditions, which may include equations and inequalities.

Radical
Radical is the symbol used to indicate the nth root of a number

Segment
In geometry, a line segment is a part of a line that is bounded by two end points, and contains every point on the line between its end points.

Radius
In classical geometry, a radius of a circle or sphere is any line segment from its center to its boundary. By extension, the radius of a circle or sphere is the length of any such segment. The radius is half the diameter. In science and engineering the term radius of curvature is commonly used as a synonym for radius.

Sector
A circular sector or circle sector also known as a pie piece is the portion of a circle enclosed by two radii and an arc.

Central
Central is an adjective usually refering to being in the centre.

Circle
In Euclidean geometry, a circle is the set of all points in a plane at a fixed distance, called the radius, from a given point, the center.

Radian
The radian is a unit of plane angle. It is represented by the symbol "rad" or, more rarely, by the superscript c (for "circular measure"). For example, an angle of 1.2 radians would be written "1.2 rad" or "1.2c" (second symbol can produce confusion with centigrads).

Hyperbola
In mathematics, a hyperbola is a type of conic section defined as the intersection between a right circular conical surface and a plane which cuts through both halves of the cone.

Torus
In geometry, a torus is a surface of revolution generated by revolving a circle in three dimensional space about an axis coplanar with the circle, which does not touch the circle. Examples of tori include the surfaces of doughnuts and inner tubes. A circle rotated about a chord of the circle is called a torus in some contexts, but this is not a common usage in mathematics. The shape produced when a circle is rotated about a chord resembles a round cushion. Torus was the Latin word for a cushion of this shape.

Rational
In mathematics, a rational number is a number which can be expressed as a ratio of two integers. Non-integer rational numbers (commonly called fractions) are usually written as the vulgar fraction a / b, where b is not zero.

Rational function
In mathematics, a rational function is any function which can be written as the ratio of two polynomial functions.

Partial fraction
In algebra, the partial fraction decomposition or partial fraction expansion is used to reduce the degree of either the numerator or the denominator of a rational function.

Shell method
shell method is a means of calculating the volume of a solid of revolution, when integrating along an axis perpendicular to the axis of revolution.

Quotient
In mathematics, a quotient is the end result of a division problem. It can also be expressed as the number of times the divisor divides into the dividend.

Numerator
A numerator is a numeral used to indicate a count. The most common use of the word today is to name the part of a fraction that tells the number or count of equal parts.

Go to **Cram101.com** for the Practice Tests for this Chapter.

Denominator	A denominator is the part of a fraction that tells how many equal parts make up a whole, and which is used in the name of the fraction: "halves", "thirds", "fourths" or "quarters", "fifths" and so on.
Greater than	In mathematics, an inequality is a statement about the relative size or order of two objects. For example 14 > 10, or 14 is greater than 10.
Multiplication	In mathematics, multiplication is an elementary arithmetic operation. When one of the numbers is a whole number, multiplication is the repeated sum of the other number.
Decomposing	decomposing refers to the reduction of the body of a formerly living organism into simpler forms of matter.
Methods for finding	There are two simple methods for finding the greatest common factor and least common multiple: standard factorization and prime factorization.
Mixed number	A mixed number is the sum of a whole number and a proper fraction.
Arithmetic	Arithmetic or arithmetics is the oldest and most elementary branch of mathematics, used by almost everyone, for tasks ranging from simple daily counting to advanced science and business calculations.
Differential	A differential is traditionally an infinitesimally small change in a variable.
Differential equation	A differential equation is a mathematical equation for an unknown function of one or several variables which relates the values of the function itself and of its derivatives of various orders.
Rationalizing	Rationalizing, or Rationalisation in mathematics is the process of removing a square root or imaginary number from the denominator of a fraction.
Exponentiating	Exponentiating is a mathematical operation, written a^n, involving two numbers, the base a and the exponent n.
Exponentiation	Exponentiation is a mathematical operation, written a^n, involving two numbers, the base a and the exponent n.
Mean	The mean, the average in everyday English, which is also called the arithmetic mean (and is distinguished from the geometric mean or harmonic mean). The average is also called the sample mean. The expected value of a random variable, which is also called the population mean.
Definite integral	definite integral is an extension of the concept of a sum.
Estimating	The act of Estimating is the calculated approximation of a result which is usable even if input data may be incomplete, uncertain, or noisy.
Trapezoid	A trapezoid is a quadrilateral, which is defined as a shape with four sides, which has a pair of parallel sides.
Numerical integration	Numerical integration constitutes a broad family of algorithms for calculating the numerical value of a definite integral, and by extension, the term is also sometimes used to describe the numerical solution of differential equations.
Rectangle	In geometry, a rectangle is defined as a quadrilateral where all four of its angles are right angles.
Parabola	In mathematics, the parabola is a conic section generated by the intersection of a right circular conical surface and a plane parallel to a generating straight line of that surface. It can also be defined as locus of points in a plane which are equidistant from a given point.

Go to **Cram101.com** for the Practice Tests for this Chapter.

Midpoint	midpoint is the middle point of a line segment.
Collinear	Three or more points that lie on the same line are called collinear.
Degenerate	In mathematics, a degenerate case is a limiting case in which a class of object changes its nature so as to belong to another, usually simpler, class.
Trapezoidal Rule	Trapezoidal Rule the American term is a way to approximately calculate the definite integral
Rounding	Rounding is the process of reducing the number of significant digits in a number.
Theoretical	In mathematics, the word theoretical is used informally to refer to certain distinct bodies of knowledge about mathematics.
Reasoning	Deductive reasoning is the kind of reasoning in which the conclusion is necessitated by, or reached from, previously known facts (the premises).
Numerical analysis	numerical analysis is the study of algorithms for the problems of continuous mathematics as distinguished from discrete mathematics.
Inequality	In mathematics, an inequality is a statement about the relative size or order of two objects.
Check	A check is a negotiable instrument instructing a financial institution to pay a specific amount of a specific currency from a specific demand account held in the maker/depositor face=symbol>¢s name with that institution. Both the maker and payee may be natural persons or legal entities.
Linear	The word linear comes from the Latin word linearis, which means created by lines.
Riemann sum	Riemann sum is a method for approximating the values of integrals.
Error function	In mathematics, the error function also called the Gauss error function is a non-elementary function which occurs in probability, statistics and partial differential equations.
Engineering	Engineering is the design, analysis, and/or construction of works for practical purposes.
Statistics	Statistics is a mathematical science pertaining to the collection, analysis, interpretation or explanation, and presentation of data. It is applicable to a wide variety of academic disciplines, from the physical and social sciences to the humanities.
Probability	Probability is the chance that something is likely to happen or be the case.
Exponential growth	In mathematics, exponential growth occurs when the growth rate of a function is always proportional to the function's current size.
Pendulum	A pendulum is an object that is attached to a pivot point so that it can swing freely.
Boundaries	In topology, the boundaries are subsets S of a topological space X is the set of points which can be approached both from S and from the outside of S.
Linear equation	A linear equation is an equation in which each term is either a constant or the product of a constant times the first power of a variable.
Constant of integration	In calculus, the indefinite integral of a given function i.e. the set of all antiderivatives of the function is always written with a constant, the constant of integration.
Integrating factor	integrating factor is a function that is chosen to facilitate the solving of a given ordinary differential equation.Consider an ordinary differential equation of the form
Coterminal	Initial objects are also called coterminal, and terminal objects are also called final.
Initial condition	In mathematics, in the field of differential equations, an initial value problem is a differential equation together with specified value, called the initial condition, of the unknown function at a given point in the domain of the solution.

Go to **Cram101.com** for the Practice Tests for this Chapter.

Mathematical model	A mathematical model is an abstract model that uses mathematical language to describe the behavior of a system. Eykhoff defined a mathematical model as 'a representation of the essential aspects of an existing system which presents knowledge of that system in usable form'.
Newton	Sir Isaac Newton, was an English physicist, mathematician, astronomer, natural philosopher, and alchemist, regarded by many as the greatest figure in the history of science
Proportional	In mathematics, two quantities are called proportional if they vary in such a way that one of the quantities is a constant multiple of the other, or equivalently if they have a constant ratio.
Temperature	Temperature is a physical property of a system that underlies the common notions of hot and cold; something that is hotter has the greater temperature.
Proportionality	Proportionality is a special mathematical relationship between two quantities.Two quantities are called proportional if they vary in such a way that one of the quantities is a constant multiple of the other, or equivalently if they have a constant ratio.
Manufacturing	Manufacturing is the application of tools and a processing medium to the transformation of raw materials into finished goods for sale.
Gallon	U.S. liquid gallon is legally defined as 231 cubic inches, and is equal to 3.785411784 litres or abotu 0.13368 cubic feet. This is the most common definition of a gallon. The U.S. fluid ounce is defined as 1/128 of a U.S. gallon.
Amount	amount is a kind of property which exists as magnitude or multitude. It is among the basic classes of things along with quality, substance, change, and relation.
Gravitational force	Gravitational force is the weakest of the four fundamental forces of bature, as described by Issac Newton
Force	In physics, force is an influence that may cause an object to accelerate. It may be experienced as a lift, a push, or a pull. The actual acceleration of the body is determined by the vector sum of all forces acting on it, known as net force or resultant force.
Velocity	Velocity of an object is its speed in a particular direction.
Opposite	In mathematics, the additive inverse, or opposite of a number n is the number that, when added to n, yields zero. The additive inverse of n is denoted −n. For example, 7 is −7, because 7 + (−7) = 0, and the additive inverse of −0.3 is 0.3, because −0.3 + 0.3 = 0.
Additive inverse	In mathematics, the additive inverse of a number n is the number that, when added to n, yields zero. The additive inverse of n is denoted −n. For example, 7 is −7, because 7 + (−7) = 0, and the additive inverse of −0.3 is 0.3, because −0.3 + 0.3 = 0.
Voltage	Voltage is the difference of electrical potential between two points of an electrical or electronic circuit, expressed in volts
Inductance	The ratio of the magnetic flux to the current is called the inductance, or more accurately self-inductance of the circuit.
Minutes	Minutes are a measure of time.
Population	In sociology and biology a population is the collection of people or organisms of a particular species living in a given geographic area or space, usually measured by a census.
Population growth	Population growth is change in population over time, and can be quantified as the change in the number of individuals in a population per unit time.
Nonlinear	nonlinear systems represent systems whose behavior is not expressible as a sum of the behaviors of its descriptors.

Plane	In mathematics, a plane is a two-dimensional manifold or surface that is perfectly flat.
Plane curve	In mathematics, a plane curve is a curve in a Euclidian plane. The most frequently studied types are the smooth plane curve, and the algebraic plane curve.
Horizontal	In astronomy, geography, geometry and related sciences and contexts, a plane is said to be horizontal at a given point if it is locally perpendicular to the gradient of the gravity field, i.e., with the direction of the gravitational force at that point.
Initial value problem	initial value problem is a differential equation together with specified value, called the initial condition, of the unknown function at a given point in the domain of the solution.
Projectile motion	Projectile motion is the path a moving object follows through space.
Slope	Slope is often used to describe the measurement of the steepness, incline, gradient, or grade of a straight line. The slope is defined as the ratio of the "rise" divided by the "run" between two points on a line, or in other words, the ratio of the altitude change to the horizontal distance between any two points on the line.
Orthogonal	In mathematics, orthogonal is synonymous with perpendicular when used as a simple adjective that is not part of any longer phrase with a standard definition. It means at right angles. It comes from the Greek á½€Ï Î¸ÏŒÏ, orthos, meaning "straight", used by Euclid to mean right; and Î³Ï‰Î½Î¯Î± gonia, meaning angle. Two streets that cross each other at a right angle are orthogonal to one another.
Orthogonal trajectory	In mathematics, a orthogonal trajectory is a family of curves in the plane that intersect a given family of curves at right angles.
Right angle	In geometry and trigonometry, a right angle is defined as an angle between two straight intersecting lines of ninety degrees, or one-quarter of a circle.
Expression	An expression is a combination of numbers, operators, grouping symbols and/or free variables and bound variables arranged in a meaningful way which can be evaluated..
Ellipse	In mathematics, an ellipse .
Compound	Compound interest refers to the fact that whenever interest is calculated, it is based not only on the original principal, but also on any unpaid interest that has been added to the principal.
Acceleration	Acceleration is defined as the rate of change or derivative with respect to time of velocity.
Kilogram	The kilogram or kilogramme is the SI base unit of mass. It is defined as being equal to the mass of the international prototype of the kilogram.
Meter	The metre (or meter, see spelling differences) is a measure of length. It is the basic unit of length in the metric system and in the International System of Units (SI), used around the world for general and scientific purposes.
Square	In plane geometry, a square is a polygon with four equal sides, four right angles, and parallel opposite sides. In algebra, the square of a number is that number multiplied by itself.
Transcendental	In mathematics, a transcendental number is a real or complex number which is not algebraic, that is, not a solution of a non-zero polynomial equation, with rational coefficients.
Asymptote	An asymptote is a straight line or curve A to which another curve B approaches closer and closer as one moves along it. As one moves along B, the space between it and the asymptote A becomes smaller and smaller, and can in fact be made as small as one could wish by going far enough along. A curve may or may not touch or cross its asymptote. In fact, the curve may

Go to **Cram101.com** for the Practice Tests for this Chapter.

intersect the asymptote an infinite number of times.

Extreme value   The term extreme value refers to the largest and the smallest element of a set.

Concavity   The word concavity means curving in or hollowed inward.

Period   In business, particularly accounting, a period is the time intervals that the accounts, statement, payments, or other calculations cover.

Sample   sample is a subset of a population.

Translation	In Euclidean geometry, a translation is moving every point a constant distance in a specified direction.
Proof	In mathematics, a proof is a demonstration that, assuming certain axioms, some statement is necessarily true.
Origin	In mathematics, the origin of a coordinate system is the point where the axes of the system intersect.
Parabola	In mathematics, the parabola is a conic section generated by the intersection of a right circular conical surface and a plane parallel to a generating straight line of that surface. It can also be defined as locus of points in a plane which are equidistant from a given point.
Perpendicular	In geometry, two lines or planes if one falls on the other in such a way as to create congruent adjacent angles. The term may be used as a noun or adjective. Thus, referring to Figure 1, the line AB is the perpendicular to CD through the point B.
Right circular cone	right circular cone is a three-dimensional geometric shape formed by straight lines through a fixed point vertex to the points of a fixed curve directrix.
Plane	In mathematics, a plane is a two-dimensional manifold or surface that is perfectly flat.
Cone	A cone is a three-dimensional geometric shape formed by straight lines through a fixed point (vertex) to the points of a fixed curve (directrix)
Conic	In mathematics, a conic section is a curve that can be formed by intersecting a cone with a plane.
Intersection	In mathematics, the intersection of two sets A and B is the set that contains all elements of A that also belong to B (or equivalently, all elements of B that also belong to A), but no other elements.
Ellipse	In mathematics, an ellipse .
Hyperbola	In mathematics, a hyperbola is a type of conic section defined as the intersection between a right circular conical surface and a plane which cuts through both halves of the cone.
Circle	In Euclidean geometry, a circle is the set of all points in a plane at a fixed distance, called the radius, from a given point, the center.
Axis	An axis is a straight line around which a geometric figure can be rotated.
Orientation	In mathematics, an orientation on a real vector space is a choice of which ordered bases are "positively" oriented, or right-handed, and which are "negatively" oriented, or left-handed.
Intersecting	In geometry, intersecting lines are two lines that share one or more common points.
Vertex	In geometry, a vertex is a special kind of point, usually a corner of a polygon, polyhedron, or higher dimensional polytope. In the geometry of curves a vertex is a point of where the first derivative of curvature is zero. In graph theory, a vertex is the fundamental unit out of which graphs are formed
Coordinate	A coordinate is a set of numbers that designate location in a given reference system, such as x,y in a planar coordinate system or an x,y,z in a three-dimensional coordinate system.
Axes	An axes is when two lines intersect somewhere on a plane creating a right angle at intersection
Horizontal	In astronomy, geography, geometry and related sciences and contexts, a plane is said to be horizontal at a given point if it is locally perpendicular to the gradient of the gravity field, i.e., with the direction of the gravitational force at that point.

Go to Cram101.com for the Practice Tests for this Chapter.

Units	The units of measurement are a globally standardized and modernized form of the metric system.
Curve	In mathematics, the concept of a curve tries to capture the intuitive idea of a geometrical one-dimensional and continuous object. A simple example is the circle.
Principle	A principle signifies a point or points of probability on a subject e.g., the principle of creativity, which allows for the formation of rule or norm or law by interpretation of the phenomena events that can be created.
Reflection	In mathematics, a reflection (also spelled reflexion) is a map that transforms an object into its mirror image.
Light	Light is electromagnetic radiation with a wavelength that is visible to the eye (visible light) or, in a technical or scientific context, electromagnetic radiation of any wavelength.
Incidence	In geometry, the relations of incidence are those such as 'lies on' between points and lines (as in 'point P lies on line L'), and 'intersects face=symbol>¢ (as in 'line L_1 intersects line L_2', in three-dimensional space). That is, they are the binary relations describing how subsets meet.
Triangle	A triangle is one of the basic shapes of geometry: a polygon with three vertices and three sides which are straight line segments.
Isosceles	An Isosceles triange is a triangle with at least two sides of equal length.
Mean	The mean, the average in everyday English, which is also called the arithmetic mean (and is distinguished from the geometric mean or harmonic mean). The average is also called the sample mean. The expected value of a random variable, which is also called the population mean.
Rays	In geometry and physics, rays are half-lines that continue forever in one direction.
Rectangle	In geometry, a rectangle is defined as a quadrilateral where all four of its angles are right angles.
Tangent	In trigonometry, the tangent is a function defined as $\tan x = \sin x /_{cos}$ x. The function is so-named because it can be defined as the length of a certain segment of a tangent (in the geometric sense) to the unit circle. In plane geometry, a line is tangent to a curve, at some point, if both line and curve pass through the point with the same direction.
Tangent line	Tangent line has two distinct but etymologically-related meanings: one in geometry and one in trigonometry.
Opposite	In mathematics, the additive inverse, or opposite of a number n is the number that, when added to n, yields zero. The additive inverse of n is denoted −n. For example, 7 is −7, because 7 + (−7) = 0, and the additive inverse of −0.3 is 0.3, because −0.3 + 0.3 = 0.
Additive inverse	In mathematics, the additive inverse of a number n is the number that, when added to n, yields zero. The additive inverse of n is denoted −n. For example, 7 is −7, because 7 + (−7) = 0, and the additive inverse of −0.3 is 0.3, because −0.3 + 0.3 = 0.
Segment	In geometry, a line segment is a part of a line that is bounded by two end points, and contains every point on the line between its end points.
Latus rectum	In a conic section, the latus rectum is the chord parallel to the directrix through the focus, with the symbol 2l.

Line segment	A line segment is a part of a line that is bounded by two end points, and contains every point on the line between its end points.
Bounded	In mathematical analysis and related areas of mathematics, a set is called bounded, if it is, in a certain sense, of finite size.
Centroid	In geometry, the centroid or barycenter of an object X in n-dimensional space is the intersection of all hyperplanes that divide X into two parts of equal moment about the hyperplane
Volume	The volume of a solid object is the three-dimensional concept of how much space it occupies, often quantified numerically.
Solid	In mathematics, solid geometry was the traditional name for the geometry of three-dimensional Euclidean space — for practical purposes the kind of space we live in.
Constant	In mathematics and the mathematical sciences, a constant is a fixed, but possibly unspecified, value. This is in contrast to a variable, which is not fixed.
Equilateral	In geometry, an equilateral polygon is a polygon which has all sides of the same length.
Equilateral triangle	An Equilateral Triangle is a triangle in which all sides are of equal length.
Scale	In Euclidean geometry, a uniform scale is a linear transformation that enlargers or diminishes objects, and whose scale factor is the same in all directions. This is also called homothethy.
Greater than	In mathematics, an inequality is a statement about the relative size or order of two objects. For example 14 > 10, or 14 is greater than 10.
Foci	In geometry, the foci are a pair of special points used in describing conic sections. The four types of conic sections are the circle, parabola, ellipse, and hyperbola.
Trace	In linear algebra, the trace of an n-by-n square matrix A is defined to be the sum of the elements on the main diagonal of A,
Minor	In linear algebra, a minor of a matrix A is the determinant of some smaller square matrix, cut down from A.
Standard position	In geometry, standard position, or general position for a set of points, or other configuration, means the general case situation, as opposed to some more special or coincidental cases that are possible.
Center	In geometry, the center of an object is a point in some sense in the middle of the object.
Square	In plane geometry, a square is a polygon with four equal sides, four right angles, and parallel opposite sides. In algebra, the square of a number is that number multiplied by itself.
Parentheses	Parentheses, either of the curved-bracket punctuation marks that together make a set of parentheses
Asymptote	An asymptote is a straight line or curve A to which another curve B approaches closer and closer as one moves along it. As one moves along B, the space between it and the asymptote A becomes smaller and smaller, and can in fact be made as small as one could wish by going far enough along. A curve may or may not touch or cross its asymptote. In fact, the curve may intersect the asymptote an infinite number of times.
Midpoint	midpoint is the middle point of a line segment.
Radius	In classical geometry, a radius of a circle or sphere is any line segment from its center to

Go to **Cram101.com** for the Practice Tests for this Chapter.

its boundary. By extension, the radius of a circle or sphere is the length of any such segment. The radius is half the diameter. In science and engineering the term radius of curvature is commonly used as a synonym for radius.

Argument In mathematics, science including computer science, linguistics and engineering, an argument is, generally speaking, an independent variable or input to a function.

Calculation A calculation is a deliberate process for transforming one or more inputs into one or more results.

Velocity Velocity of an object is its speed in a particular direction.

Range In mathematics, the range of a function is the set of all "output" values produced by that function. Given a function f :A
$\rightarrow$ B, the range of
class="unicode">f, is defined to be the set {x
class="unicode">   B:x=
class="unicode">f(a) for some a
class="unicode">   A}.

Navigation Navigation is the process of planning, recording, and controlling the movement of a craft or vehicle from one place to another.

Product In mathematics, a product is the result of multiplying, or an expression that identifies factors to be multiplied.

Shapes Shapes are external two-dimensional outlines, with the appearance or configuration of some thing - in contrast to the matter or content or substance of which it is composed.

Eccentricity eccentricity is a parameter associated with every conic section.

Coordinate system In mathematics and its applications, a coordinate system is a system for assigning an n-tuple of numbers or scalars to each point in an n-dimensional space.

Reference A frame of reference is a particular perspective from which the universe is observed.

Polar In functional analysis and related areas of mathematics the polar set of a given subset of a vector space is a certain set in the dual space.

Frame of reference A frame of reference is a particular perspective from which the universe is observed.

Right angle In geometry and trigonometry, a right angle is defined as an angle between two straight intersecting lines of ninety degrees, or one-quarter of a circle.

Radian The radian is a unit of plane angle. It is represented by the symbol "rad" or, more rarely, by the superscript c (for "circular measure"). For example, an angle of 1.2 radians would be written "1.2 rad" or "1.2c" (second symbol can produce confusion with centigrads).

Ray A ray given two distinct points A and B on the ray, is the set of points C on the line containing points A and B such that A is not strictly between C and B.

Pairs In mathematics, the conjugate pairs or adjoint matrix of an m-by-n matrix A with complex entries is the n-by-m matrix A* obtained from A by taking the transpose and then taking the complex conjugate of each entry.

Multiple A multiple of a number is the product of that number with any integer.

Quadrant A Quadrant consists of one quarter of the coordinate plane.

Integers The integers are the only integral domain whose positive elements are well-ordered, and in which order is preserved by addition. Like the natural numbers, the integers form a countably

Go to **Cram101.com** for the Practice Tests for this Chapter.

infinite set. The set of all integers is usually denoted in mathematics by a boldface Z .

Sine	Sine is a trigonemtric function that is important when studying triangles and modeling periodic phenomena, among other applications.
Multiplication	In mathematics, multiplication is an elementary arithmetic operation. When one of the numbers is a whole number, multiplication is the repeated sum of the other number.
Symmetry	Symmetry means "constancy", i.e. if something retains a certain feature even after we change a way of looking at it, then it is symmetric.
Lemniscate	In mathematics, the Lemniscate of Bernoulli is an eight-shaped algebraic curve described by a Cartesian equation
Cosine	The cosine of an angle is the ratio of the length of the adjacent side to the length of the hypotenuse.
Law of cosines	The law of cosines is a statement about a general triangle which relates the lengths of its sides to the cosine of one of its angles.
Test	Acid test ratio measures the ability of a company to use its near cash or quick assets to immediately extinguish its current liabilities.
Closed curve	In mathematics, a closed curve is a connected curve that does not intersect itself and ends at the same point in which it starts.
Period	In business, particularly accounting, a period is the time intervals that the accounts, statement, payments, or other calculations cover.
Function	The mathematical concept of a function expresses the intuitive idea of deterministic dependence between two quantities, one of which is viewed as primary and the other as secondary. A function then is a way to associate a unique output for each input of a specified type, for example, a real number or an element of a given set.
Interval	In elementary algebra, an interval is a set that contains every real number between two indicated numbers and may contain the two numbers themselves.
Extreme value	The term extreme value refers to the largest and the smallest element of a set.
Curves	In mathematics, curves are the intuitive idea of a geometrical one-dimensional and continuous object.
Cardioid	In geometry, the cardioid is an epicycloid with one cusp. That is, a cardioid is a curve that can be produced as the path of a point on the circumference of a circle as that circle rolls around another fixed circle with the same radius.
Rotation	A rotation is a movement of an object in a circular motion. A two-dimensional object rotates around a center (or point) of rotation. A three-dimensional object rotates around a line called an axis. If the axis of rotation is within the body, the body is said to rotate upon itself, or spin—which implies relative speed and perhaps free-movement with angular momentum. A circular motion about an external point, e.g. the Earth about the Sun, is called an orbit or more properly an orbital revolution.
Convex	A convex function curves downwards. The graph of a convex function of one variable remains above its tangents and below its cords.
Limagon	In mathematics, a limagon is a heart-shaped mathematical curve. The cardioid is considered a special case, with a cusp.
Inner loop	In computer programs, an important form of control flow is the inner loop.
Magnitude	The magnitude of a mathematical object is its size: a property by which it can be larger or

smaller than other objects of the same kind; in technical terms, an ordering of the class of objects to which it belongs.

Valid
In statistics, a valid measure is one which is measuring what is supposed to measure.

Distribution
In mathematical analysis, distribution are objects which generalize functions and probability distributions.

Potential
In physics, a potential may refer to the scalar potential or to the vector potential.

Force
In physics, force is an influence that may cause an object to accelerate. It may be experienced as a lift, a push, or a pull. The actual acceleration of the body is determined by the vector sum of all forces acting on it, known as net force or resultant force.

Graphs
Graphs are the basic objects of study in graph theory. Informally speaking, a graph is a set of objects called points, nodes, or vertices connected by links called lines or edges.

Conjecture
In mathematics, a conjecture is a mathematical statement which appears likely to be true, but has not been formally proven to be true under the rules of mathematical logic.

Sector
A circular sector or circle sector also known as a pie piece is the portion of a circle enclosed by two radii and an arc.

Central
Central is an adjective usually refering to being in the centre.

Inequality
In mathematics, an inequality is a statement about the relative size or order of two objects.

Boundaries
In topology, the boundaries are subsets S of a topological space X is the set of points which can be approached both from S and from the outside of S.

Continuous
A continuous function is a function for which, intuitively, small changes in the input result in small changes in the output.

Partition
Generally, a partition is a splitting of something into parts.

Integration
Integration is a process of combining or accumulating. It may also refer to:

Strophoid
Strophoid is a cubic curve generated by increasing or diminishing the radius vector of a variable point Q on a straight line AB by the distance QC of the point from the foot of the perpendicular drawn from the origin to the fixed line.

Real number
In mathematics, a real number may be described informally as a number that can be given by an infinite decimal representation.

Half-space
Half-space is either of the two parts into which a plane divides the three-dimensional space. More generally, a half-space is either of the two parts into which a hyperplane divides an affine space.

Arc
In Euclidean geometry, an arc is a closed segment of a differentiable curve in the two-dimensional plane; for example, a circular arc is a segment of a circle.

Domain
In mathematics, a domain of a k-place relation L ⊆ X_1 × ... × X_k is one of the sets X_j, $1 \leq j \leq k$. In the special case where k = 2 and L ⊆ X_1 class="unicode">× X_2 is a function L : X_1 class="unicode">→ X_2, it is conventional to refer to X_1 as the domain of the function and to refer to X_2 as the codomain of the function.

Identity
An identity is an equality that remains true regardless of the values of any variables that appear within it, to distinguish it from an equality which is true under more particular conditions.

Parameter	A parameter is the quantity that defines certain relatively constant characteristics of systems or functions..
Travel	Travel is the transport of people on a trip/journey or the process or time involved in a person or object moving from one location to another.
Perpetuity	A perpetuity is an annuity that has no definite end, or a stream of cash payments that continues forever.
Check	A check is a negotiable instrument instructing a financial institution to pay a specific amount of a specific currency from a specific demand account held in the maker/depositor face=symbol>¢s name with that institution. Both the maker and payee may be natural persons or legal entities.
Linear	The word linear comes from the Latin word linearis, which means created by lines.
Unit circle	Unit circle is a circle with a unit radius, i.e., a circle whose radius is 1.
Lissajous	In mathematics, a Lissajous curve is the graph of the system of parametric equations, which describes complex harmonic motion.
Parametric	Parametric statistics are statistics that estimate population parameters.
Parametric equations	In mathematics, parametric equations bear slight similarity to functions: they allow one to use arbitrary values, called parameters, in place of independent variables in equations, which in turn provide values for dependent variables. A simple kinematical example is when one uses a time parameter to determine the position, velocity, and other information about a body in motion.
Simplifying	In mathematics, simplifying expressions is used to reduce the expression into the lowest possible term.
Calculus	Calculus is a mathematical subject that includes the study of limits, derivatives, integrals, and power series and constitutes a major part of modern university curriculum.
Galileo Galilei	Galileo Galilei was an Italian physicist, mathematician, astronomer, and philosopher who is closely associated with the scientific revolution.
Projectile	A projectile is any object propelled through space by the applicationp of a force.
Projectile motion	Projectile motion is the path a moving object follows through space.
Acceleration	Acceleration is defined as the rate of change or derivative with respect to time of velocity.
Measure	A measure is a function that assigns a number to subsets of a given set.
Coterminal	Initial objects are also called coterminal, and terminal objects are also called final.
Theoretical	In mathematics, the word theoretical is used informally to refer to certain distinct bodies of knowledge about mathematics.
Experiment	In the scientific method, an experiment (Latin: ex-+-periri, "of (or from) trying"), is a set of actions and observations, performed in the context of solving a particular problem or question, in order to support or falsify a hypothesis or research concerning phenomena.
Slope	Slope is often used to describe the measurement of the steepness, incline, gradient, or grade of a straight line. The slope is defined as the ratio of the "rise" divided by the "run" between two points on a line, or in other words, the ratio of the altitude change to the horizontal distance between any two points on the line.
Transformation	In mathematics, a transformation in elementary terms is any of a variety of different functions from geometry, such as rotations, reflections and translations.

Quadratic formula	A quadratic equation with real solutions, called roots, which may be real or complex, is given by the quadratic formula: $x = \frac{-b \pm \sqrt{b^2 - 4ac}}{2a}$.
Union	In set theory and other branches of mathematics, the union of a collection of sets is the set that contains everything that belongs to any of the sets, but nothing else.
Finite	In mathematics, a set is called finite if there is a bijection between the set and some set of the form $\{1, 2, ..., n\}$ where n is a natural number.
Derivative	The derivative is a measurement of how a function changes when the values of its inputs change.
Sum	A sum is the result of the addition of a set of numbers. The numbers may be natural numbers, complex numbers, matrices, or still more complicated objects. An infinite sum is a subtle procedure known as a series.
Arc length	Arc length also called rectification of a curve—was historically difficult.
Theorem	In mathematics, a theorem is a statement that can be proved on the basis of explicitly stated or previously agreed assumptions.
Consecutive	Consecutive means in succession or back-to-back
Integral	The integral of a function is an extension of the concept of a sum, and are identified or found through the use of integration.
Riemann sum	Riemann sum is a method for approximating the values of integrals.
Circumference	The circumference is the distance around a closed curve. Circumference is a kind of perimeter.
Chain rule	In calculus, the chain rule is a formula for the derivative of the composite of two functions.
Plane curve	In mathematics, a plane curve is a curve in a Euclidian plane. The most frequently studied types are the smooth plane curve, and the algebraic plane curve.
Rate	A rate is a special kind of ratio, indicating a relationship between two measurements with different units, such as miles to gallons or cents to pounds.
Endpoint	In geometry, an endpoint is a point at which a line segment or ray terminates.
Image	In mathematics, image is a part of the set theoretic notion of function.
Descartes	Descartes was a highly influential French philosopher, mathematician, scientist, and writer. Dubbed the "Founder of Modern Philosophy", and the "Father of Modern Mathematics". His theories provided the basis for the calculus of Newton and Leibniz, by applying infinitesimal calculus to the tangent line problem, thus permitting the evolution of that branch of modern mathematics
Integrand	Integrand is a function that extends the concept of an ordinary sum
Antiderivative	An antiderivative of a function f is a function F whose derivative is equal to f, i.e., $F' = f$.
Catenary	Catenary is the shape of a hanging flexible chain or cable when supported at its ends and acted upon by a uniform gravitational force. The chain is steepest near the points of suspension because this part of the chain has the most weight pulling down on it. Toward the bottom, the slope of the chain decreases because the chain is supporting less weight.

Sphere	In mathematics, a sphere is the set of all points in three-dimensional space (R^3) which are at distance r from a fixed point of that space, where r is a positive real number called the radius of the sphere. The fixed point is called the center or centre, and is not part of the sphere itself.
Differential calculus	Differential calculus, a field in mathematics, is the study of how functions change when their inputs change. The primary object of study in differential calculus is the derivative.
Variable	A variable is a symbolic representation denoting a quantity or expression. It often represents an "unknown" quantity that has the potential to change.
Center of mass	In physics, the center of mass of a system of particles is a specific point at which, for many purposes, the system's mass behaves as if it were concentrated.
Mass	Mass is the property of a physical object that quantifies the amount of matter and energy it is equivalent to.
Axis of symmetry	Axis of symmetry of a two-dimensional figure is a line such that, if a perpendicular is constructed, any two points lying on the perpendicular at equal distances from the axis of symmetry are identical.
Newton	Sir Isaac Newton, was an English physicist, mathematician, astronomer, natural philosopher, and alchemist, regarded by many as the greatest figure in the history of science
Leibniz	Leibniz was a German mathematician and philosopher. He invented calculus independently of Newton, and his notation is the one in general use since.
Definite integral	definite integral is an extension of the concept of a sum.
Slant height	The slant height of a right circular cone is the distance from any point on the circle to the apex of the cone.
Lateral	A lateral surface is the surface or face of a solid on its sides. It can also be defined as any face or surface that is not a base.
Ring	In mathematics, a ring is an algebraic structure in which addition and multiplication are defined and have properties listed below.
Cycloid	A cycloid is the curve defined by the path of a point on the edge of circular wheel as the wheel rolls along a straight line.
Planes	In mathematics, planes are two-dimensional manifolds or surfaces that are perfectly flat.
Ellipsoid	An ellipsoid is a type of quadric surface that is a higher dimensional analogue of an ellipse.
Density	Density is mass m per unit volume V.
Torus	In geometry, a torus is a surface of revolution generated by revolving a circle in three dimensional space about an axis coplanar with the circle, which does not touch the circle. Examples of tori include the surfaces of doughnuts and inner tubes. A circle rotated about a chord of the circle is called a torus in some contexts, but this is not a common usage in mathematics. The shape produced when a circle is rotated about a chord resembles a round cushion. Torus was the Latin word for a cushion of this shape.
Friction	Friction is the force that opposes the relative motion or tendency toward such motion of two surfaces in contact.
Gravitational force	Gravitational force is the weakest of the four fundamental forces of bature, as described by Issac Newton

Go to Cram101.com for the Practice Tests for this Chapter.

Harmonic	In acoustics and telecommunication, the harmonic of a wave is a component frequency of the signal that is an integer multiple of the fundamental frequency.
Harmonic motion	Simple harmonic motion is the motion of a simple harmonic oscillator, a motion that is neither driven nor damped. Complex harmonic motion is the superposition — linear combination — of several simultaneous simple harmonic motions.
Amount	amount is a kind of property which exists as magnitude or multitude. It is among the basic classes of things along with quality, substance, change, and relation.
Calculus of variations	Calculus of variations is a field of mathematics that deals with functionals, as opposed to ordinary calculus which deals with functions. Such functionals can for example be formed as integrals involving an unknown function and its derivatives. The interest is in extremal functions: those making the functional attain a maximum or minimum value.
Simultaneous	simultaneous is the property of two events happening at the same time in at least one reference frame.
Spirals	In mathematics, a spirals are a curve which emanates from a central point, getting progressively farther away as it revolves around the point.
Conversion	Conversion is a concept in traditional logic referring to a "type of immediate inference in which from a given proposition another proposition is inferred which has as its subject the predicate of the original proposition and as its predicate the subject of the original proposition (the quality of the proposition being retained)."
Continuous function	A continuous function is a function for which, intuitively, small changes in the input result in small changes in the output.

Interval	In a large distribution of data it is often easier to understand the data if it is grouped into intervals where each interval can contain more than one data value. Distributions are often reduced to 10 to 20 intervals.
Intervals	At times we must contend with variables that assume a large number of values. In this case it is typical to create intervals of values of the variable and then make a frequency tally of the number of observations falling within each interval. As is the case with any data reduction technique, detail is lost.
Constants	There are properties of objects that do assume one and only value, and we refer to these characteristics as constants. Constants, then, are the invariables that differentiate one class of objects from another.
Range	A measure of variability, the range is the distance from the lowest to the highest score.
Variable	The very fact that we are measuring objects with respect to some characteristic implies that the objects differ in that characteristic; or stated in another way, that the characteristic can take on a number of different values. These properties or characteristics of an object that can assume two or more different values are referred to as a variable.
Estimate	An estimate is an indication of the value of an unknown quantity based on observed data. More formally, an estimate is the particular value of an estimator that is obtained from a particular sample of data and used to indicate the value of a parameter.
Experiment	An experiment is any process or study, which results in the collection of data, the outcome of which is unknown. In statistics, the term is usually restricted to situations in which the researcher has control over some of the conditions under which the experiment takes place.
Power	The probability of correctly rejecting a false Ho is referred to as power.
Mean	The most important measure of central tendency, and one of the basic building blocks of all statistical analysis, is the arithmetic mean. It is simply the sum of all the set of values divided by the number of values involved. As a measure of central tendency, it is affected by extreme scores, and it assumes a ratio scale of measurement.
Geometric mean	A statistic calculated by multiplying the data values together and taking the N-th root of the result., the geometric mean is often used as a measure of central tendency for skewed distributions.
Generalization	The goal of most inferential statistical analyses is to be able to generalize or apply the findings to the entire population and not just to the sample. The concept of generalization requires that the researcher determine some level of probability that the findings were due to chance or that they actually describe the population. The value of the probability that the findings were due to chance is usually reported when the findings of an analysis is reported.
Constant	A number that does not change in value in a given situation is a constant.
Statistics	Statistical analysis, sometimes referred to simply as Statistics, is concerned with the definition and collection, organization, and interpretation of data according to well-defined procedures. The term itself, statistics, is a defining characteristic of a sample, such as a sample mean, or sample standard deviation.
Probability	A probability provides a quantitative description of the likely occurrence of a particular event. Probability is conventionally expressed on a scale from 0 to 1; a rare event has a probability close to 0, a very common event has a probability close to 1. Probability is calculated as the ratio of the number of favorable events to the total number of possible events.
Density	Density, the height of the curve for a given value of X; closely related to the probability

Go to **Cram101.com** for the Practice Tests for this Chapter.
And, **NEVER** highlight a book again!

of an observation in an interval around X.

Probability Density Function

The probability density function of a continuous random variable is a function, which can be integrated to obtain the probability that the random variable takes a value in a given interval.

Standard deviation

A measure of variability in a distribution, the standard deviation is the square root of the variance. The standard deviation measures the variability of scores around the mean: the standardized difference. It is the square root of the mean square error.

Deviation

A deviation refers to the distance or difference between any score in a distribution of data from the mean.

Sigma	The Greek letter sigma indicates summation.
Variable	The very fact that we are measuring objects with respect to some characteristic implies that the objects differ in that characteristic; or stated in another way, that the characteristic can take on a number of different values. These properties or characteristics of an object that can assume two or more different values are referred to as a variable.
Constant	A number that does not change in value in a given situation is a constant.
Mean	The most important measure of central tendency, and one of the basic building blocks of all statistical analysis, is the arithmetic mean. It is simply the sum of all the set of values divided by the number of values involved. As a measure of central tendency, it is affected by extreme scores, and it assumes a ratio scale of measurement.
Interval	In a large distribution of data it is often easier to understand the data if it is grouped into intervals where each interval can contain more than one data value. Distributions are often reduced to 10 to 20 intervals.
Intervals	At times we must contend with variables that assume a large number of values. In this case it is typical to create intervals of values of the variable and then make a frequency tally of the number of observations falling within each interval. As is the case with any data reduction technique, detail is lost.
Estimate	An estimate is an indication of the value of an unknown quantity based on observed data. More formally, an estimate is the particular value of an estimator that is obtained from a particular sample of data and used to indicate the value of a parameter.
Weighted average	By weighted average we mean an average calculated by taking into account not only the frequencies of the values of a variable but also some other factor such as their variance. The weighted average of observed data is the result of dividing the sum of the products of each observed value, the number of times it occurs, and this other factor by the total number of observations
Sample	A sample is a subset or portion of a population. Samples are extremely important in the field of statistical analysis, since due to economic and practical constraints we usually cannot make measurements on every single member of the particular population.
Power	The probability of correctly rejecting a false Ho is referred to as power.
Differences	The same statistical principles apply to the evaluation of observed differences between sets of data. The field of statistics provides the necessary techniques for making statements of our certainty that there are real as opposed to chance differences.
Binomial	A binomial is simply a polynomial with two terms.
Generalization	The goal of most inferential statistical analyses is to be able to generalize or apply the findings to the entire population and not just to the sample. The concept of generalization requires that the researcher determine some level of probability that the findings were due to chance or that they actually describe the population. The value of the probability that the findings were due to chance is usually reported when the findings of an analysis is reported.
Constants	There are properties of objects that do assume one and only value, and we refer to these characteristics as constants. Constants, then, are the invariables that differentiate one class of objects from another.
Slope	The slope refers to the amount of change in Y for a 1 unit change in X; or in-other-words, the rate of change in the predicted value as a function of a change in the predictor variable.

Go to **Cram101.com** for the Practice Tests for this Chapter.

Go to **Cram101.com** for the Practice Tests for this Chapter.
And, **NEVER** highlight a book again!

Scale	A scale is a scheme for the numerical representation of the values of a variable. The interpretation we place upon the numbers of the scale, rather than the numbers themselves, makes the scale useful. The most common scales are nominal, ordinal, interval
Symmetry	Symmetry is implied when data values are distributed in the same way above and below the middle of the sample.
Midpoint	The midpoint is often confused with the median. The Median is a statistic for the distribution whereas the midpoint provides a statistic for an interval; it is the center of the interval; the arithmetic average of the upper and lower limits.
Factor	Factor is used synonymously for variable.
Mean	The most important measure of central tendency, and one of the basic building blocks of all statistical analysis, is the arithmetic mean. It is simply the sum of all the set of values divided by the number of values involved. As a measure of central tendency, it is affected by extreme scores, and it assumes a ratio scale of measurement.
Constant	A number that does not change in value in a given situation is a constant.
Generalization	The goal of most inferential statistical analyses is to be able to generalize or apply the findings to the entire population and not just to the sample. The concept of generalization requires that the researcher determine some level of probability that the findings were due to chance or that they actually describe the population. The value of the probability that the findings were due to chance is usually reported when the findings of an analysis is reported.
Power	The probability of correctly rejecting a false Ho is referred to as power.
Parameter	A parameter is a value used to represent a certain population characteristic. Because of the impracticality of measuring an entire population to determine this value, parameters are usually estimated.
Parameters	The defining characteristics of populations are called parameters. Observations must be made on every single member of the population in question in order to precisely state the value of parameters.
Intercept	The value of Y when X is 0 is the intercept.

Go to **Cram101.com** for the Practice Tests for this Chapter.
And, **NEVER** highlight a book again!

Interval	In a large distribution of data it is often easier to understand the data if it is grouped into intervals where each interval can contain more than one data value. Distributions are often reduced to 10 to 20 intervals.
Constant	A number that does not change in value in a given situation is a constant.
Constants	There are properties of objects that do assume one and only value, and we refer to these characteristics as constants. Constants, then, are the invariables that differentiate one class of objects from another.
Experiment	An experiment is any process or study, which results in the collection of data, the outcome of which is unknown. In statistics, the term is usually restricted to situations in which the researcher has control over some of the conditions under which the experiment takes place.
Parameter	A parameter is a value used to represent a certain population characteristic. Because of the impracticality of measuring an entire population to determine this value, parameters are usually estimated.
Range	A measure of variability, the range is the distance from the lowest to the highest score.
Mean	The most important measure of central tendency, and one of the basic building blocks of all statistical analysis, is the arithmetic mean. It is simply the sum of all the set of values divided by the number of values involved. As a measure of central tendency, it is affected by extreme scores, and it assumes a ratio scale of measurement.
Estimate	An estimate is an indication of the value of an unknown quantity based on observed data. More formally, an estimate is the particular value of an estimator that is obtained from a particular sample of data and used to indicate the value of a parameter.
Slope	The slope refers to the amount of change in Y for a 1 unit change in X; or in-other-words, the rate of change in the predicted value as a function of a change in the predictor variable.
Data	By data we mean collecting observations made upon our environment -- observations, which are the results of measurements using clocks, balances, measuring rods, counting operations, or other objectively defined measuring instruments or procedures. Data may mean simply counting the number of times a particular property occurs.
Objects	Objects refer to any data source, whether individuals, physical or biological things, geographic locations, time periods, or events; that is, anything upon which observations can be made.
Power	The probability of correctly rejecting a false Ho is referred to as power.

Go to **Cram101.com** for the Practice Tests for this Chapter.

Variables	Variables are characteristics or properties of an object that can take on one or more different values.
Range	A measure of variability, the range is the distance from the lowest to the highest score.
Variable	The very fact that we are measuring objects with respect to some characteristic implies that the objects differ in that characteristic; or stated in another way, that the characteristic can take on a number of different values. These properties or characteristics of an object that can assume two or more different values are referred to as a variable.
Constant	A number that does not change in value in a given situation is a constant.
Interval	In a large distribution of data it is often easier to understand the data if it is grouped into intervals where each interval can contain more than one data value. Distributions are often reduced to 10 to 20 intervals.
Constants	There are properties of objects that do assume one and only value, and we refer to these characteristics as constants. Constants, then, are the invariables that differentiate one class of objects from another.
Symmetry	Symmetry is implied when data values are distributed in the same way above and below the middle of the sample.
Experiment	An experiment is any process or study, which results in the collection of data, the outcome of which is unknown. In statistics, the term is usually restricted to situations in which the researcher has control over some of the conditions under which the experiment takes place.
Mean	The most important measure of central tendency, and one of the basic building blocks of all statistical analysis, is the arithmetic mean. It is simply the sum of all the set of values divided by the number of values involved. As a measure of central tendency, it is affected by extreme scores, and it assumes a ratio scale of measurement.
Slope	The slope refers to the amount of change in Y for a 1 unit change in X; or in-other-words, the rate of change in the predicted value as a function of a change in the predictor variable.
Generalization	The goal of most inferential statistical analyses is to be able to generalize or apply the findings to the entire population and not just to the sample. The concept of generalization requires that the researcher determine some level of probability that the findings were due to chance or that they actually describe the population. The value of the probability that the findings were due to chance is usually reported when the findings of an analysis is reported.
Probability	A probability provides a quantitative description of the likely occurrence of a particular event. Probability is conventionally expressed on a scale from 0 to 1; a rare event has a probability close to 0, a very common event has a probability close to 1. Probability is calculated as the ratio of the number of favorable events to the total number of possible events.

Go to **Cram101.com** for the Practice Tests for this Chapter.

Variable	The very fact that we are measuring objects with respect to some characteristic implies that the objects differ in that characteristic; or stated in another way, that the characteristic can take on a number of different values. These properties or characteristics of an object that can assume two or more different values are referred to as a variable.
Variables	Variables are characteristics or properties of an object that can take on one or more different values.
Interval	In a large distribution of data it is often easier to understand the data if it is grouped into intervals where each interval can contain more than one data value. Distributions are often reduced to 10 to 20 intervals.
Differences	The same statistical principles apply to the evaluation of observed differences between sets of data. The field of statistics provides the necessary techniques for making statements of our certainty that there are real as opposed to chance differences.
Slope	The slope refers to the amount of change in Y for a 1 unit change in X; or in-other-words, the rate of change in the predicted value as a function of a change in the predictor variable.
Density	Density, the height of the curve for a given value of X; closely related to the probability of an observation in an interval around X.
Constant	A number that does not change in value in a given situation is a constant.
Parameter	A parameter is a value used to represent a certain population characteristic. Because of the impracticality of measuring an entire population to determine this value, parameters are usually estimated.
Distribution	In statistics an arrangement of values of a variable showing their observed or theoretical frequency of occurrence is called a distribution.
Mean	The most important measure of central tendency, and one of the basic building blocks of all statistical analysis, is the arithmetic mean. It is simply the sum of all the set of values divided by the number of values involved. As a measure of central tendency, it is affected by extreme scores, and it assumes a ratio scale of measurement.
Estimate	An estimate is an indication of the value of an unknown quantity based on observed data. More formally, an estimate is the particular value of an estimator that is obtained from a particular sample of data and used to indicate the value of a parameter.
Data	By data we mean collecting observations made upon our environment -- observations, which are the results of measurements using clocks, balances, measuring rods, counting operations, or other objectively defined measuring instruments or procedures. Data may mean simply counting the number of times a particular property occurs.
Least Squares	The method of least squares is a criterion for fitting a specified model to observed data.
Geometric mean	A statistic calculated by multiplying the data values together and taking the N-th root of the result., the geometric mean is often used as a measure of central tendency for skewed distributions.
Measurement	Measurement is the result of assigning numbers to objects to abstractly represent the objects or characteristics of the objects.
Upper limit	In a distribution of data or in an interval of data, the upper limit is the greatest value.
Range	A measure of variability, the range is the distance from the lowest to the highest score.

Go to **Cram101.com** for the Practice Tests for this Chapter.

Mean	The most important measure of central tendency, and one of the basic building blocks of all statistical analysis, is the arithmetic mean. It is simply the sum of all the set of values divided by the number of values involved. As a measure of central tendency, it is affected by extreme scores, and it assumes a ratio scale of measurement.
Constants	There are properties of objects that do assume one and only value, and we refer to these characteristics as constants. Constants, then, are the invariables that differentiate one class of objects from another.
Factors	Another word for independent variables in the analysis of variance is factors.
Sigma	The Greek letter sigma indicates summation.
Constant	A number that does not change in value in a given situation is a constant.
Interval	In a large distribution of data it is often easier to understand the data if it is grouped into intervals where each interval can contain more than one data value. Distributions are often reduced to 10 to 20 intervals.
Estimate	An estimate is an indication of the value of an unknown quantity based on observed data. More formally, an estimate is the particular value of an estimator that is obtained from a particular sample of data and used to indicate the value of a parameter.
Symmetry	Symmetry is implied when data values are distributed in the same way above and below the middle of the sample.
Variables	Variables are characteristics or properties of an object that can take on one or more different values.
Midpoint	The midpoint is often confused with the median. The Median is a statistic for the distribution whereas the midpoint provides a statistic for an interval; it is the center of the interval; the arithmetic average of the upper and lower limits.
Probability	A probability provides a quantitative description of the likely occurrence of a particular event. Probability is conventionally expressed on a scale from 0 to 1; a rare event has a probability close to 0, a very common event has a probability close to 1. Probability is calculated as the ratio of the number of favorable events to the total number of possible events.
Distribution	In statistics an arrangement of values of a variable showing their observed or theoretical frequency of occurrence is called a distribution.
Density	Density, the height of the curve for a given value of X; closely related to the probability of an observation in an interval around X.
Objects	Objects refer to any data source, whether individuals, physical or biological things, geographic locations, time periods, or events; that is, anything upon which observations can be made.
Factor	Factor is used synonymously for variable.
Range	A measure of variability, the range is the distance from the lowest to the highest score.
Variable	The very fact that we are measuring objects with respect to some characteristic implies that the objects differ in that characteristic; or stated in another way, that the characteristic can take on a number of different values. These properties or characteristics of an object that can assume two or more different values are referred to as a variable.
Abscissa	The abscissa is another name for the horizontal axis of a graph or plot.
Ordinate	The ordinate is the vertical axis of a graph.

Go to **Cram101.com** for the Practice Tests for this Chapter.

Linear transformation	A linear transformation involves the addition, subtraction, multiplication, or division of one variable by another variable or by a constant.
Generalization	The goal of most inferential statistical analyses is to be able to generalize or apply the findings to the entire population and not just to the sample. The concept of generalization requires that the researcher determine some level of probability that the findings were due to chance or that they actually describe the population. The value of the probability that the findings were due to chance is usually reported when the findings of an analysis is reported.
Weighted average	By weighted average we mean an average calculated by taking into account not only the frequencies of the values of a variable but also some other factor such as their variance. The weighted average of observed data is the result of dividing the sum of the products of each observed value, the number of times it occurs, and this other factor by the total number of observations

Density	Density, the height of the curve for a given value of X; closely related to the probability of an observation in an interval around X.
Constant	A number that does not change in value in a given situation is a constant.
Parameter	A parameter is a value used to represent a certain population characteristic. Because of the impracticality of measuring an entire population to determine this value, parameters are usually estimated.
Interval	In a large distribution of data it is often easier to understand the data if it is grouped into intervals where each interval can contain more than one data value. Distributions are often reduced to 10 to 20 intervals.
Estimate	An estimate is an indication of the value of an unknown quantity based on observed data. More formally, an estimate is the particular value of an estimator that is obtained from a particular sample of data and used to indicate the value of a parameter.
Factor	Factor is used synonymously for variable.
Variable	The very fact that we are measuring objects with respect to some characteristic implies that the objects differ in that characteristic; or stated in another way, that the characteristic can take on a number of different values. These properties or characteristics of an object that can assume two or more different values are referred to as a variable.
Differences	The same statistical principles apply to the evaluation of observed differences between sets of data. The field of statistics provides the necessary techniques for making statements of our certainty that there are real as opposed to chance differences.
Power	The probability of correctly rejecting a false Ho is referred to as power.
Symmetry	Symmetry is implied when data values are distributed in the same way above and below the middle of the sample.
Dummy variable	A special case of the dichtomous variable is the dummy variable which is created by converting a level of a qualitative variable into a binary variable.
Variables	Variables are characteristics or properties of an object that can take on one or more different values.
Range	A measure of variability, the range is the distance from the lowest to the highest score.
Experiment	An experiment is any process or study, which results in the collection of data, the outcome of which is unknown. In statistics, the term is usually restricted to situations in which the researcher has control over some of the conditions under which the experiment takes place.
Distribution	In statistics an arrangement of values of a variable showing their observed or theoretical frequency of occurrence is called a distribution.
Mean	The most important measure of central tendency, and one of the basic building blocks of all statistical analysis, is the arithmetic mean. It is simply the sum of all the set of values divided by the number of values involved. As a measure of central tendency, it is affected by extreme scores, and it assumes a ratio scale of measurement.
Depth	By depth we mean the cumulative frequency, counting in from the nearer end.
Interaction	In a factorial design with two or more main effects or grouping effects, there is a possibility of a significant interaction effect, AB. With a significant interaction you have differences in estimates of the population variance in the various combinations, or cells, of one main effect paired with another. Interactions must be explained before main effects in a statistical analysis. The interaction is tested using an F test in an ANOVA that compares the MSab/Mserror.

Go to **Cram101.com** for the Practice Tests for this Chapter.
And, **NEVER** highlight a book again!

Weighted average	By weighted average we mean an average calculated by taking into account not only the frequencies of the values of a variable but also some other factor such as their variance. The weighted average of observed data is the result of dividing the sum of the products of each observed value, the number of times it occurs, and this other factor by the total number of observations

Go to **Cram101.com** for the Practice Tests for this Chapter.

Constant	A number that does not change in value in a given situation is a constant.
Constants	There are properties of objects that do assume one and only value, and we refer to these characteristics as constants. Constants, then, are the invariables that differentiate one class of objects from another.
Variables	Variables are characteristics or properties of an object that can take on one or more different values.
Interval	In a large distribution of data it is often easier to understand the data if it is grouped into intervals where each interval can contain more than one data value. Distributions are often reduced to 10 to 20 intervals.
Variable	The very fact that we are measuring objects with respect to some characteristic implies that the objects differ in that characteristic; or stated in another way, that the characteristic can take on a number of different values. These properties or characteristics of an object that can assume two or more different values are referred to as a variable.
Estimate	An estimate is an indication of the value of an unknown quantity based on observed data. More formally, an estimate is the particular value of an estimator that is obtained from a particular sample of data and used to indicate the value of a parameter.
Slope	The slope refers to the amount of change in Y for a 1 unit change in X; or in-other-words, the rate of change in the predicted value as a function of a change in the predictor variable.
Weighted average	By weighted average we mean an average calculated by taking into account not only the frequencies of the values of a variable but also some other factor such as their variance. The weighted average of observed data is the result of dividing the sum of the products of each observed value, the number of times it occurs, and this other factor by the total number of observations
Experiment	An experiment is any process or study, which results in the collection of data, the outcome of which is unknown. In statistics, the term is usually restricted to situations in which the researcher has control over some of the conditions under which the experiment takes place.
Factors	Another word for independent variables in the analysis of variance is factors.
Factor	Factor is used synonymously for variable.
Mean	The most important measure of central tendency, and one of the basic building blocks of all statistical analysis, is the arithmetic mean. It is simply the sum of all the set of values divided by the number of values involved. As a measure of central tendency, it is affected by extreme scores, and it assumes a ratio scale of measurement.
Parameters	The defining characteristics of populations are called parameters. Observations must be made on every single member of the population in question in order to precisely state the value of parameters.
Frequency	The number of times a particular score or observation occurs is its frequency.
Event	The outcome of a trial is called the event.
Density	Density, the height of the curve for a given value of X; closely related to the probability of an observation in an interval around X.

CPSIA information can be obtained at www.ICGtesting.com

230883LV00001B/76/A

9 781428 834507